The Reference Shelf (Continued)

Volume XII. $6

No.
1. Anglo-American Agreement. H. B. Summers. $1.25.
2. Discussion Methods Explained and Illustrated. J. V. Garland and C. F. Phillips. (rev. ed. 1940) $1.25.
3. The State Sales Tax. E. R. Nichols and others. $1.25.
4. Dictatorships vs. Democracies. 1938 (Supplement to Anglo-American Agreements) H. B. Summers and R. E. Summers. 75c.

No.
5. Pump-priming Theory of Government Spending. E. R. Nichols and William E. Roskam. $1.25.
6. United States Foreign Policy: Isolation or Alliance. J. E. Johnsen. $1.25.
7. Chain Stores and Legislation. Daniel Bloomfield. $1.25.
8. The United States and War. J. E. Johnsen.
9. Debate Index. E. M. Phelps. 75c.
10. Radio Censorship. H. B. Summers. $1.25.

Volume XI. $6

No.
1. Unicameral Legislatures. H. B. Summers.
2. Consumers' Cooperatives. J. E. Johnsen, J. V. Garland, C. F. Phillips.
3. Industrial versus Craft Unionism. J. E. Johnsen.
4. Reorganization of the Supreme Court. J. E. Johnsen.
5. Unicameralism in Practice: The Nebraska Legislative System. H. B. Summers.

No.
6. Modern Group Discussion. L. and E. Judson.
7. Arbitration and the National Labor Relations Board. E. R. Nichols and J. W. Logan.
8. Peace and Rearmament. J. E. Johnsen.
9. Chinese-Japanese War, 1937-. J. E. Johnsen.
10. Representative American Speeches: 1937-1938. A. C. Baird. $1.25.

Volume X. $4.20

No.
1. Collective Bargaining. J. E. Johnsen.
2. Lotteries. H. M. Muller.
3. Old Age Pensions. J. E. Johnsen.
5. Socialization of Medicine. J. E. Johnsen.

No.
6. Limitation of Power of Supreme Court to Declare Acts of Congress Unconstitutional. J. E. Johnsen.
9. Government Ownership of Electric Utilities. J. E. Johnsen.
10. The Crisis in the Electric Utilities. Garland and Phillips.

ST. THOMAS COLLEGE
LIBRARY

THE REFERENCE SHELF

Vol. 15   No. 9

PERMANENT PRICE CONTROL POLICY

Compiled by
JULIA E. JOHNSEN

THE H. W. WILSON COMPANY
NEW YORK   1942

Copyright 1942
by The H. W. Wilson Company
All Rights Reserved
Published August 1942

PRINTED IN THE UNITED STATES OF AMERICA

PREFACE

The Emergency Price Control Act of 1942 became law on January 30th, to remain in effect until June 30, 1943 unless terminated previously, or extended. Its six months of administration, similarly to the period preceding its adoption, has been productive of much discussion and public concern.

Stressed as an essential anti-inflation measure and a vital concomitant of wartime defense, price control has presented a succession of problems and aspects. Among the more outstanding of these, the question of selective or over-all controls, was placed on a new basis with the promulgation, on April 28th, of the General Maximum Price Regulation, following a seven-point program offered on the previous day by the President, which was designed to meet increasing inflationary trends and persistent price rises. In this period, also, the extension of controls to agricultural prices, rents and wages underwent widespread discussion. Still more recently has arisen the question of subsidies, a large appropriation being sought from Congress so that price ceilings might be supported by extensive financial contributions to industry.

This number of the Reference Shelf is supplementary to *Federal Price Control* (Reference Shelf Volume 15, number 4, published January 1942) and brings down to date new discussions and bibliographical references appearing since the former publication. In addition it has sought to bring out available discussions looking to price control as a policy of more permanent interest than that having to do with the Act as it now stands. With the approach of the expiration of this Act the issue will doubtless be more immediately joined as to its abrogation or its extension; its extension either as to a new arbitrary point of time, or its retension, in line with the experience following the First World War, for a definite period after the war to

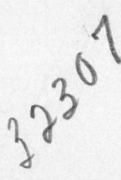

safeguard the transition of our economy under reconstruction. Finally also there is the question whether some form of government price control should be retained permanently, as a fundamental principle of a new socio-economic order, an order envisaged by many as affording the possibility of a more widespread stability and concern for the common welfare than has characterized our pre-war world.

In keeping with the established policy of the series, material is presented impartially from varied points of view. The wage aspect has been extensively covered in a recent number of the Reference Shelf, *Wages and Prices* by Robert E. Summers, published in April.

Acknowledgment is gratefully made to various publications and authors for courtesies extended in granting the use of copyright materials.

JULIA E. JOHNSEN

July 30, 1942

CONTENTS

Preface 3

Discussion 7

Lerner, Max. Economic Strategy in a Democracy ....
.... New Republic 7

Wardwell, Charles A. R. and Matchett, Gerald J. Price Ceilings and Wartime Control Over American Economy ....
.... Survey of Current Business 14

Hirsch, Julius. Some Effects of Price Control ..... Barron's 20

Mitchell, Walter, Jr. Six Biggest Snags in the Path of Price Control .... Sales Management 27

Anderson, Benjamin M. Price-Fixing and Commodity Control .... Economic Bulletin 34

Waite, Warren C. Price Fixing of Agricultural Products
.... American Statistical Association Journal 40

Consequences of Inflation .... Federal Reserve Bulletin 47

America in Revolution .... Christian Century 50

Sumner, John D. Effects of the War on Price Policies ....
.... American Economic Review 55

Arnold, Thurman W. Proposed Organization for Prevention of Unjustified Price Increases 59

Spahr, Walter E. Program for the War and for the Years To Follow .... Controller 62

Harris, Seymour E. Wartime Price Control and the Americas
.... Foreign Commerce Weekly 66

Anti-Inflation Program ....
..... American Federation of Labor Weekly News Service 69

Emergency Price-Control Act ...... Monthly Labor Review 72

Excerpts 79

BIBLIOGRAPHY 99

DISCUSSION

ECONOMIC STRATEGY IN A DEMOCRACY [1]

To be part of the national government today means, as like as not, to be in the thick of economics. We speak of the movement away from laissez-faire, as if that disposed of the future. It only opens its problems. Every economic system in the world has moved beyond laissez-faire, as it has moved beyond the water-wheel and hand weaving. What distinguishes one system from another is the strategy for economic control it has adopted.

Willy-nilly, the task of every government in our time has become the choice of economic strategies. And this has had to be an active, rather than a passive, choice. W. H. Auden has remarked, with his new fatalism, that we do not live: we are lived. That may be true of the person; it dare not be true of the collectivity. In the negative state our political scientists evolved the concept of "pressure politics"—the pressures applied by special-interest groups on the government. In the affirmative state we must replace it by the concept of "economic strategies"—the strategies directed by the government toward the mechanisms of the economy. What distinguishes a democracy from other governments is this: that not only must it make the choices among available strategies, but those choices must be made in response to the life needs of the people as a whole; and having made the choice, the government must find power and administrative methods for enforcing it, educational methods for explaining it and methods of controlling the controllers so that the choice will not sacrifice freedom to order.

One way of looking at economic strategies is to define the role that the government plays. From the eighties on, when

[1] By Max Lerner, Professor of Political Science. Williams College. *New Republic*. 106:856-8. June 22, 1942.

state public-service commissions first began on a large scale to fix utility rates and the Interstate Commerce Commission began to take the railroad problem seriously, the government has been regulator. With Theodore Roosevelt and Woodrow Wilson, with the campaign of trust-busting and the use of the Federal Reserve discount process, the government became controller. And with the movement for conservation of resources at the turn of the century, and notably with the T.V.A. and the Board of Economic Warfare, we have taken the initial steps toward planning.

The lines between these three functions—regulation, control, planning—are obviously not sharply drawn. But the division is worth making. In the first, the government acts as umpire or arbiter, to administer the rules of the game, but takes no part in determining the plays. In the second, the government is one of the participants, throwing the weight of its power now in one direction, now in another: it is more than umpire but less than manager. In the third the government is manager: it has by no means crowded out the other players; but it plans, or helps plan, the broad and decisive moves.

But while this tells us something of the government's role, it does not tell us about the economic material it must work with. Some of the best of recent American economic thinking, under the spur of the need for governmental control, has been on the nature of the "market" economy we have. The group around Vice President Wallace while he was Secretary of Agriculture, particularly Gardiner Means and Mordecai Ezekiel, saw that we had in reality a price structure "half of steel and half of putty"—some of the prices, as in aluminum, cement, automobiles, rigid and unresponsive to changes in demand; others, as in agriculture and coal, all too responsive.

During the decades from the eighties the Big Stick had to be wielded against unresponsive monopolies, and we learned painfully some aspects of the trust problem, with its system of rigid prices set regardless of the public good. But in the

PERMANENT PRICE CONTROL POLICY

Great Depression anti-trust was ignored and even suspended. The threatening trend seemed to be widespread price collapse among the "putty" prices, in industries where no one competitor or group could dominate the market. Hence came the N.R.A. in the consumers' goods and durable-goods industries, the Petroleum Administration in crude oil production, the Bituminous Coal Commission and the A.A.A. All of these served their emergency purpose at the time. Some have died without any to lament them, some have been scrapped by the Supreme Court only to be revived. But it is worth noting that in none has any real solution been reached of the basic problem of excess capacity and collapsing prices.

For the moment the war economy has obscured our failure to find a solution, but the failure is there none the less. In agriculture the enormous new demands that our armies and allies are making, the new domestic market opened by war employment, and the post-war needs from devastated areas will all have changed the picture for a generation. Nevertheless, although for the moment the farmers are worrying about a ceiling on farm prices, the enduring strategy of placing a floor below them by restricting production and regulating the pace of its entrance into the market remains unchanged. While Louis Hacker was surely hasty in announcing in 1933 that "the farmer is doomed," one can still agree with the note of pessimism in Carey McWilliams' *Ill Fares the Land*, with its cutting analysis of the ravages wrought by technology, factory farms and land-tenure systems, and its implication that the health of agriculture is inseparable from that of the rest of the economy.

Much the same analysis could be made of oil and coal. Price-and-production control has been necessary but not adequate. The technics of crude-oil production have combined with the archaic logic of the legal system and the predatory ethos of capitalism to turn the oil industry into a jungle of greed, piracy and competitive violence. In the twenties the system of control by state governments through the "proration" method proved a dismal failure. Since that time the supplementary federal control of "hot oil" production and below-cost prices under the Connally Acts has been a patchwork affair, just tolerable enough to enable the oil producers to kill any plan—such as the recent one of the National Resources Committee—which aims primarily at engineering efficiency and oil conservation. In coal, chronically depressed since the First World War, the strategy since the days of the N.R.A. has been to set minimum prices to keep the industry from collapsing, and at the same time to freeze against change the basic structure of competing producers and producing areas. This has meant the administering of aid at once by pulmotor and refrigeration. And again the solution, while no answer for the long run, has been just tolerable enough to avoid facing the complete socialization of coal, such as was recommended in the twenties by the Sankey Commission in England, and such as the English have only now begun to approach.

I know that no conclusions can merge from a few industrial instances. But actually we have adequate studies now of the price-and-production structure of most industries. I do not want to underestimate the complexity of the "market" factors uncovered by these studies. One may say that our economists have given up Alfred Marshall's quest for the "normal" industrial plant and have resigned themselves to the "unique" industrial situation. But the fact that no two industries are exactly alike does not mean that there can be no common strategies of control which could be adapted to each situation.

The strategies I have cited have had one principle in common—and that the wrong one. Because they have been unwilling to face the need for government planning and changed ownership relations, they have moved not toward full employment and the maximizing of national income, but toward the stabilizing of prices and wages under a contracting economy. Given the initial lack of will to grapple boldly with the problem, such a result could probably not have been avoided. But we ought to recognize it for what it is. There has been a good deal of recent writing about the need for a return to the "free market." But the ironic thing about the industries I have been discussing is that in them the market has been free, all too free. The more responsible "free market" writers have made reservations in such cases, and have tended to accept the strategies in use. But they are caught in a dilemma. If, in order to get stability of prices, they accept the freezing of competitive relations, they lose the quality of "business initiative" that they so have celebrated. And if, in their quest of freedom, they remove the props the government has set up under prices and wages, they get industrial chaos.

Let us move now from the markets that need government strategies because they are all too free, to the markets that need them because they are not free enough. I shall not labor here the well known work of Thorstein Veblen, of Brandeis, of Berle and Means and of the government investigations from Pujo to Pecora into the economic effects of corporate and financial concentrations. Enough to sum them up by saying what is now not seriously disputed—that it has meant the sabotaging of full production and employment, the growth of a state within a state, in Thurman Arnold's phrase, "the private seizure of industrial power." The economists, with unintentional irony, call it "imperfect competition," and spend their energy classifying and analyzing the varieties and degrees of imperfection.

The traditional American approach in the face of these facts has been one of trust-busting, pursued with less vigor than clangor. Thurman Arnold's now famous chapter on the anti-trust laws in his *Folklore of Capitalism* tells brilliantly how we managed to reconcile making a big noise with doing nothing. Now, in the Anti-Trust Division, he has chosen to discard not the noise but the inaction. Through his increased staff, which has combined economic with legal research, and through his new use of the grand-jury indictment, he has had some effect. His method has been strategic rather than punitive: not to convict people, but to use the threat of conviction to pry sticky prices loose and break the "bottlenecks" in the way of full production.

But there are lumps even in the very modern anti-trust porridge of Mr. Arnold, as Alan Sweezy pointed out in these pages some weeks ago. I leave aside for the moment the difficult question of his strategy toward trade-union practices. More serious is his reliance upon judicial procedures to tame a structure of economic power to the uses of the community—as evidenced by the recent decision in the Aluminum case. The fact is that, except for the Supreme Court itself, the federal judiciary is today little more competent than ever to deal with the whole range of economic problems, and little more inclined to forsake the corporate hare for the New Deal hound. And as for Congress, while Mr. Arnold's labor utterances and suits have given him a standing with congressmen not far below that of Jesse Jones, this amiability becomes a distant and frozen smile as soon as Mr. Arnold brings up the question of war contracts and cartel agreements and patent control.

The anti-trust campaign has not had easy going since America moved into a war economy. On the one hand it has had to face the stubborn, if well meant, opposition of the War and Navy Departments personnel, which has found it easier to deal with a few big companies than with many small ones, and which is not too loath to get immediate delivery even at the expense of greater rigidity of monopoly power. On the other hand anti-trust has been frightened off by the prospect of interminable litigation, and has had therefore to accept the terms laid down by the corporate lawyers as part of the consent decrees. Unable to use its administrative and court machinery, anti-trust has had to content itself with a publicity campaign against the firms which have used their patent monopolies to obstruct war production, and which have clung to cartel arrangements with German corporations in the Nazi command economy. But here too Mr. Arnold and his staff have met the glacial indifference of the congressional reactionaries and the studied neglect of the press.

Mr. Arnold is not a man to be disheartened even by a solid phalanx of opposition. He has been saying recently that the post-war period will be one of prosperity rather than depression. If he means that we can have prosperity if we know how to go about it, he is quite right, and far sounder in his emphasis than the former isolationists, like Norman Thomas and O. G. Villard, who now have turned their energies into depicting an economically stricken post-war America. But if he means that anti-trust alone can release these productive energies for us, he is allowing his buoyancy to get the better of his realism.

For we shall have to deal after the war, as during the war, with the structure of industrial obstruction formed by the combination of corporate interests, congressional spokesmen and press mercenaries. And in doing so we shall need far more than anti-trust and the grand-jury indictment. The monographs prepared during the past four years under the T.N.E.C. come closer to pointing the way toward full employment than do any of the strategies I have discussed so far. So also does the strategy of using governmental expenditures to make up for the "normal" stagnation of investment, as embodied in the thinking of the American branch of the Keynesian school under Alvin Hansen and the group of young New Deal economists around him. So also does the experience we have had in attempting to plan the war economy, and the directives for the future that this experience has given us.

To these themes I want to address myself in a further article. The growing point of economic strategy in a democracy is today no longer the N.R.A. attempt to stabilize a contracting economy by propping up prices and wages, nor the refurbished attempt to slay the trust dragon by the St. George of the restraint-of-trade concept. It lies rather in new fiscal and new planning strategies. The war has shown that the economic machine can be put to full use if the military emergency compels us to do so. The problem now is to achieve by act of collective will what has been forced on us by the compulsions of Mars.

PRICE CEILINGS AND WARTIME CONTROL OVER AMERICAN ECONOMY [2]

During World War I, a previous generation of federal administrators grappled with the inflation problem and invoked price controls. These, however, were of the selective type. Only prices of materials basic to the nation's food, fuel, and munitions supply were singled out for restraint. In all, 573 commodities were brought under government control by various agencies at some time during the war, most of them at the manufacturers' or wholesalers' level. These controls began during the summer of 1917 and lasted until December 31, 1918. They were effective, as long as they were operative, in promoting reasonable stability among the controlled prices. The uncontrolled goods, of course, were free to rise. They did so, rising nearly one-fourth during the year and a half of price control, and accounting for the entire price level rise in this period. After controls were removed, prices generally resumed their uneven rise until the postwar inflation peak in 1920. Of the total wartime inflation, roughly six-tenths occurred before price controls were instituted, about one-tenth while they were in effect, and the other three-tenths after controls were removed.

The General Maximum Price Regulation is unique, therefore, not in its application of price controls to the American economy but rather for its sweeping character. Not just 573 prices as in World War I but, with notable exceptions, all goods and many services; not just at wholesale but also at retail. If the number of retail establishments now in business is substantially the same as at the time of the 1939 Census, there are

[2] By Charles A. R. Wardwell and Gerald J. Matchett. *Survey of Current Business.* 22:19-26. June, 1942.

approximately 1,800,000. For most of the numerous individual articles offered at retail in each of these establishments there is a price ceiling. The ceilings on the same article will differ from one establishment to the others. These retailers will buy from roughly 200,000 wholesalers who in turn will buy from approximately 180,000 manufacturing establishments. Each wholesaler has a ceiling price on each article he handles and likewise each manufacturer has a ceiling price on each article he makes and sells. Thus there are literally tens of millions of ceiling prices and profit margins and 2 million business establishments with various problems growing out of price relations—vital problems which may determine whether each one of them stays in business or not—now firmly ensconced on the doorstep of the Office of Price Administration.

The significant features of the current price level situation will escape any observer who fails to realize that they are merely one part of the whole problem of economic mobilization for war. Hence before discussing the problems of price control as such, we shall gain perspective if we first orientate ourselves with reference to some of the fundamentals of the program for total economic mobilization.

Total war—for survival—means that a maximum proportion of all the economic resources of the nation must be brought to bear against our enemies in both defense and offense. This means the arraying for war purposes of a maximum proportion of our natural resources, of our manpower, and of our capital equipment. No household can escape participation in one way or another in the common effort.

The overshadowing economic problem is production: a maximum of war goods for the armed forces and the remainder—a residual as large as practicable—for civilians. Vast war expenditures by the government are necessary. These create several closely inter-related subsidiary problems: that of raising revenues, that of averting inflation as the floodtide of consumer purchasing power is confronted by a diminishing supply of consumer goods, that of rationing scarce goods equitably, and others. But the supply problem always comes first—ample supplies for the fighting forces and as ample as can be for civilians. To accomplish this, the government is bound to take any necessary measures to ensure that adequate quantities of materials, of labor, and of management flow into the war industries, largely out of civilian lines. Whether this conversion of the economy is achieved by the hope of profit, by patriotism, or by some sort of compulsion, it must be done.

Prior to the General Maximum Price Regulation, the government built up the war industries chiefly by ordering cessation or limitation of civilian goods output, and by priorities and the allocation of materials and equipment. Other means of fostering these industries were, increasingly, allocation of transportation, of fuel and of power. Price control, from this viewpoint, and quite in addition to its power to check inflation, is also another instrument for the government to use in mastering the basic problem of wartime supply and mobilization. It enables the government to hitch to economic mobilization the basic functions of the price mechanism as it operated under free enterprise.

One vital function the price system helped to perform was to guide the flow of capital, materials, labor, and management into alternative fields of endeavor. Price changes, as these influenced profits, were perhaps the chief factor determining the relative quantities in which various goods and services were produced. High or rising prices were an invitation to productive factors to move into a given field to increase output there. Low or falling prices tended to divert productive resources and thus discourage production. In those fields not subject to superior controls, prices will still function in this manner.

For some months, however, the flow of materials and equipment has been guided to an increasing extent by the War Production Board. From now on the flow of labor will be increasingly subject to the War Manpower Commission. Prices and profit margins will still guide the flow of productive resources not otherwise guided—but the prices set will be subject to the jurisdiction of the Office of Price Administration. Accordingly this agency can adjust profit margins favorably in cases where it wishes to encourage output or distribution, and squeeze the margins in cases where it is necessary in the national interest to discourage the output and sale of an article.

Another vital function of prices was to guide consumption. Low prices were an invitation to purchase more, and high prices, less, of any given article. Hence both the choice of goods and the amounts purchased by individual consumers, were determined by prices on the basis of ability to pay. Prices will still influence consumer choices, but they will increasingly be those prices set by the Price Administrator rather than by market decisions. And the quantities consumed per person, at least in the case of scarce articles, will be determined by O.P.A. ration regulations as well as by ability to pay.

Hence in one way or another, various government agencies have either assumed the traditional functions of the price system or will supplant them by more direct controls over production and consumption. The same development has already taken place in Great Britain, Russia, Germany, and other warring nations. Our economy cannot otherwise be effectively mobilized for total war.

The Emergency Price Control Act of 1942, whence come most of the government's powers over prices, set forth nine broad objectives as the purpose of the act. Prevention of inflation is one major goal specified. Another is the assuring of adequate production. A third is to prevent dissipation of defense appropriations by excessive prices. Price control broadly viewed, therefore, can be considered as one of the most important measures—but only one of them—available to the government for effecting economic mobilization for war and for distributing equitably over all groups in the community the costs and sacrifices necessary to the nation's war effort.

It is fully to be expected, therefore, that the government will exercise its control over prices to prevent inflation as completely as possible, directly or indirectly to encourage certain types of production and discourage others, and also to encourage certain types of consumption while discouraging other types.

Most of the concern about inflation seems to have focused on the cost of living. Our estimates (admittedly rough) indicate that in the year ending June 30, 1943, the federal government alone will purchase about as many goods and services as will be available to the entire body of civilian consumers. Within a short time, therefore, the Office of Price Administration expects to bring an important share of the government's purchases under formal control.

The exact nature of all of the companion measures that must operate along with price regulation in the joint mobilization efforts has not been determined. What these forthcoming measures must do, however, is abundantly clear. First, they must mop up most of the consumer purchasing power over and above the amounts needed to buy the available supplies of consumer goods and services at their ceiling prices or less. This will be accomplished by higher taxes collected in one way or another from consumers and also by much larger purchases of war bonds by consumers out of their current incomes. The more adequate these fiscal measures are to effect this purpose, the less will be the pressure against the price ceilings and the simpler will be the enforcement problem of the Office of Price Administration.

Secondly, other measures will be needed to stabilize the prices so far exempted from control. Some of these exemptions threaten cost-of-living stabilization, such as prices of personal services and food consumed in eating places. Others threaten the cost of doing business, such as wages and salaries. Whatever may be the measures designed to prevent the further rise of these and other exempted items, it is clear that they must rest upon fundamental criteria which are themselves solidly rooted in broad social policy. Involved, of course, is the whole question of the distribution of the national income and the standards of living of the various groups in the community in wartime.

Another companion measure needed to supplement price control in wartime management of the standard of living is the rationing of all scarce goods and services. This is inevitable as obviously it would be contrary to the national welfare to permit the first few people in line, on the first-come first-served basis, to buy up most of the available supply and leave only remnants for the others. There is one special aspect of rationing important enough to mention in passing. This is the need for rationing of inventories of scarce goods among distributors. Unless this is done, grave problems of maldistribution of merchandise among mercantile outlets and between different localities may arise to disrupt the equitable flow of scarce goods to consumers.

Price control and the reduction of the unit volume of consumer goods will bring profound changes in the distributive trades. The variety of goods offered for sale will diminish. Some commodities will disappear from the market completely. Fewer services will be offered in connection with the sale of commodities. Whereas formerly distributors competed with one another for consumer trade, competition may now be just as intense in the struggle to obtain merchandise. The consumer will be less well served.

For the duration, manufacturers and distributors of consumers' goods will be a less significant element in the total economy. Failures and retirements among them will increase. Those manufacturers who can shift to war goods will suffer very little save during the immediate adjustment period. While cases of individual hardship are bound to be numerous, portions of the labor and resources released will be available for use in war industries. Thus part of the losses suffered by consumer goods manufacturers, distributors, and their employees will be a gain to the war economy.

While many of the major cost-of-living prices may be stabilized, the standard of living is bound to fall. Civilian production will be severely curtailed. Accumulated inventories will be drawn down. In addition, there is likely to be considerable deterioration in the quality of commodities and some further advance in commodity prices.

In its fundamental policy-making decisions, the O.P.A. will in fact be faced with three principal alternatives. The authorities may decide that quality deterioration is preferable to allowing an advance in price. Or they may further decide that price ceilings can be held by removing or diminishing the upward pressure of rising costs. To accomplish this end, they may refuse to grant relief to marginal concerns who will then be forced out of business. This will cut output of the goods concerned but will also free labor and materials and thus check the tendency for these cost prices to rise. Or finally, rather than sacrifice quality or output, the authorities may decide to grant relief through either some form of subsidy or an increase in the price ceiling.

Such price advances as do occur, however, will unquestionably be at a slower rate. How fast and how much the rise is, will depend largely upon the energy with which the remainder of the President's program is put into effect. If the rise is to be a minimum, the necessary measures must be adopted to remove surplus purchasing power and to stabilize prices of goods and services not now subject to the March ceilings. The battle against inflation is essentially a battle with many fronts. Hence it can be lost by a break through on some unguarded front.

SOME EFFECTS OF PRICE CONTROL [3]

Unsolved, the questions of farm prices and wages will cause severe maladjustments in costs of production. Such maladjust-

[3] By Julius Hirsch, in charge of Germany's Price Control Board in the latter part of World War I. *Barron's.* 22:3. May 11, 1942.

ments may ultimately have to be remedied by the granting of subsidies to assist enterprises which find themselves the victims of disproportionately inflated costs. However, let us first look at the immediate consequences of the general price order.

1. Licensing has now been authorized on a comprehensive scale. As of May 18, most retail and wholesale establishments will be licensed. Newcomers will also have to register, and it is estimated that a total of two million enterprises will be affected. It should also be noted that many concerns will have to obtain three or even more licenses: One for retail or wholesale, another for instalment business; and many must be "authorized dealers" to distribute a rationed or allocated commodity. Additional licenses must be had for specified commodities.

2. With a decreasing volume of civilian commodities in the offing, most probably accompanied by a rise of the spendable purchasing power in the hands of consumers, there will be a strong tendency toward a widening of rationing and allocations. Since ceilings prevent price increases from curtailing consumer demand, favoritism among customers tends to become a fine and remunerative art on the part of the seller, with the consequence that available goods are distributed inequitably. This is bound to give rise to dissatisfaction and denunciation of responsible authorities. The obvious solution lies in the government's assuming responsibility for equal distribution. It will be seen, therefore, that what started out as a "mere" matter of government price fixing, becomes by sheer necessity government control over distribution extended over the flow of goods by supervision, allocation, customer lists, and ultimately, rationing. The significance of this is obvious.

3. The price freezing order undertakes no less than the control of billions of individual prices. This attempt is to be implemented by the obligation on the part of every manufacturer, wholesaler and retailer to prepare and submit a complete list of (a) the "highest price" charged in March, 1942, for every kind of product sold and (b) the "offering price" where

a sale was not consumated. Taken into consideration must be customary discounts and other price differentials.

Stricter and more bothersome control measures are proposed with respect to the retail sale of so-called "cost-of-living commodities." In the case of such commodities, which are individually listed in the order, a price tag must be attached to the article or a price list prominently displayed so that the consumer may check on the legality of the price asked. Furthermore, retailers are obligated to file with their local War Price and Rationing Board "a statement showing his maximum price for each such commodity and a description or identification of it." Subsequently, prices for new kinds of commodities will have to be filed.

It may be assumed that at least 90 per cent, or 1.5 million, of all retail outlets will have to comply with the provision for submitting price lists. As far as small and medium sized grocery stores are concerned, it is estimated that on the average approximately 1,000 different items will have to be included in the list. Department stores may very well find that their number of customarily handled goods reaches 100,000. This will give an idea of the magnitude of the price listing to be accomplished by grocery, specialty and department stores, respectively. But, once this work is accomplished, every price charged or offered in March, 1942, can be controlled completely from then on.

At best, price control cannot do more than it says; it controls prices. However, prices are the result of an interplay of numerous cost factors and business methods, and it is patently impossible to freeze or petrify the latter. It is idle to expect a voluntary leveling out of two of the major cost factors, agricultural prices and industrial wages. Experience in foreign countries suggests that, even when a formal stabilization has been accomplished, there is still enough force left behind the claims of these two powerful groups, labor and agriculture, to result in pressure towards price increases.

PERMANENT PRICE CONTROL POLICY

Assuming that agricultural prices will soon be stabilized at some level—the present controversy is directed not at stabilization as such, but at its level—there is still reason for believing that labor will continue to demand higher wages. This means that employers will be forced to demand higher prices or other compensation. It does not take much imagination to see caravans of employers and employees, accompanied by politicians, on their way to Washington forming "coalitions" against the Price Administration.

But, assuming that the O.P.A. will be able to defeat such coalitions, there is still the problem that, if present plans are to be realized, five to six million more wage earners will have to be pressed into the active labor force of the country. This spells higher wages and greater payrolls, for there has never been a labor boom without boosts in wage rates.

Moreover, ample experience abroad has shown that even when all prices, wages, rents and profits are frozen, cost increases never can be avoided entirely. These arise partly from disturbances in traffic, rising transportation costs, the necessity of using substitutes for cheap imported commodities like rubber —and by dozens of similar deteriorations of quality and service.

The question then arises, how can this inevitable and probably strong trend be reconciled with fixed prices? Two possible answers suggest themselves: (1) Deflation of the cost structure of business and "squeezing" of various cost factors and (2) government subsidies for diverse, including "non-essential," industries. Concerning the second, one is tempted to ask: Is this country going to witness a "class struggle for subsidies?"

Let's consider first the position of retailers.

When the price freezing order was issued, retailers pointed to the varying time lag between wholesale and retail price movements, and argued that they would be squeezed unless wholesale and manufacturers' prices were "rolled back" by the amount of the lag. This problem lay behind the O.P.A.'s announcement, just three days after the general freezing order was issued that "retail prices will not be increased. The ceiling will not be punctured. . . . Adjustments may be made in manufacturers' and wholesalers' prices." However, the Price Administration made no general provision for such adjustments, but imposed on retailers the necessity of offering proof when their price margins are insufficient. This involves the laborious preparation of cost data and the process of dealing with the O.P.A.'s Retail Trade and Service Division.

There are other possible ways in which the squeeze will work.

In normal business life some commodities are usually sold without a profit or even at a loss to attract customers. If their prices cannot be raised above the level of March, 1942, who can force the business man to rebuy them at all once he has sold his stock? Such prescription would mean the administrative imposition of sales policy.

Loss leaders, being in the nature of overhead charges, cannot be continued when costs have to be curtailed, especially as they are no longer needed for competition, which tends to disappear under price control and licensing.

Other forms of competitive effort shrink under price control. Advertising is affected. Free delivery will be cut to a minimum. Credit will be restricted more and more. While the Price Administrator will always try to maintain an unchanged price for each commodity and service he will not object, and, in fact, will encourage, the "absorption" or "equalization of costs." Thus a maximum selling price may remain constant while one cost element declines and another increases.

While in principle the freezing regulation demands that the same commodity plus the same service be sold for the same price, as in March, 1942, some deterioration of standards is inevitable. A simplification of styles is already in progress. This is one form of the squeeze—and a rather harmless one. Many other forms of "rationalization"—such as reductions in numbers of sizes—are being recommended with the same purpose

PERMANENT PRICE CONTROL POLICY

in view, but the speed with which they can be realized should not be over-estimated.

Wrappings and containers will certainly become less elaborate and less elegant than before. Since the shortage of paper and other packaging material is bound to increase, it is doubtful whether the Price Administration will oppose a deterioration in this kind of service. And, almost inevitably, frozen prices will cause some deterioration in quality of goods. High quality is the child of plenty and competition. Scarcity and absence of competition are enemies of quality.

The main difficulty is the squeeze among makers, handlers and sellers in the broad field of consumers' goods.

As soon as pressure is felt there, the question of subsidies arises. England reports subsidies to the amount of £150 million (sterling) a year; Japan before going to war already had subsidies totaling 600 million yen. The United States Treasury undoubtedly must prepare for considerable outlays of this nature.

The subsidy method is used only after careful examination of the cost level and after all other possibilities have been exhausted. This leads to studies of long range methods of possible cost and profit adjustments. Many of them are closely related to the methods used for more than 40 years by European cartels. The most important ones are the following.

A natural tendency in all times of scarcity and price control is to shorten the commercial route of the commodity from the first producer to the ultimate consumer. The greatest squeeze will perhaps be on middlemen. Political and economic considerations often make it expedient to permit jobbers, commission men, agents, brokers, etc., to carry on. Need for them after the war is one consideration. However, there is a great probability that some of them will be wiped out as a result of the squeeze.

Since transportation costs are indirectly included in the price ceiling, it is very probable that long distance shipping will be avoided as much as possible. The distant buyer will have to bear the cost if he wants the commodity. The general result will be almost complete disappearance of cross hauling and an over-all saving as far as transportation is concerned.

The tendency to save transportation and distribution costs will strongly intensify the tendency towards vertical concentration of industries, whereby manufacturers control their own sources of supply. This will be further accentuated by unavoidable bottlenecks in transportation and by shortages of basic raw materials. The company which has its own mines at hand will never run short of materials. The factory built on the site of its main raw material source will always have regular occupation, while others, buying from distant places, suffer from transportation lags.

Perhaps the most important consequence of the squeeze will be the tendency to spread costs by pooling. For example, what would otherwise be a disposition to neglect badly located customers will probably be met by equalization funds for freight charges, contributed by the more fortunately situated buyers.

This may force the imposition of fixed sales quotas, and perhaps even the setting of limitations on sales areas for various business establishments.

When prices are fixed, new and ersatz commodities grow up like mushrooms under a warm rain, and their prices must be controlled too, preferably at the same level as exactly comparable commodities. If that is not possible, wholesalers and retailers generally are allowed to use the same percentage mark-up as on the fastest moving comparable commodity of the same general classification. They have only to give their calculation to O.P.A.

Manufacturers, however, have to get the permission of the O.P.A. before selling such a new article. One consequence of this procedure will be that many tens of thousands of new and ersatz commodities will have to be examined by the O.P.A. In some countries the attempt was even made to examine the qualities of such substitutes before permitting sale. There is no doubt that the handling of this one item will prove shortly to be a much bigger task than is now anticipated.

The ceiling imposed on producers' goods, especially machinery and tools, is less rigid in most countries than that imposed on consumers' goods. If a piece of new machinery can help to reduce costs of production, it does not matter very much if that machinery is 10 per cent to 15 per cent higher in price than the equipment it replaces. Price administrators abroad permit the charging of such higher prices, and some of the first exemptions permitted after issuance of the general order here referred to certain producers' goods.

In general, the adjustment of industries to price control is most difficult where business units are smallest. These are the ones in which violations and bootlegging are most likely to appear most frequently. The industries composed of big units, and the large companies in all lines, adjust themselves to the rules even if the adjustment results in losses.

But it must be remembered that no business large or small, can long continue to operate at a loss. It is quite feasible to compel a business to function at a lower profit, but never, in the long run, at a deficit.

The administration of prices we are about to witness poses an enormous task. But difficult as it will be, and many as are the hardships it will inflict, it is now a prerequisite to winning the war.

SIX BIGGEST SNAGS IN THE PATH OF PRICE CONTROL [4]

Six major problems face the O.P.A. in applying price controls. A clear understanding of them may be helpful in interpreting the daily installments of information about shortages, price and rationing problems.

[4] By Walter Mitchell, Jr., Dun and Bradstreet, Inc., New York. *Sales Management.* 50:20-2. February 15, 1942.

The six problems are:

1. *Horizontal.* The problem of fixing prices on competing commodities.

2. *Vertical.* The need for fixing prices in various neighboring stages of distribution so that one part of the business community does not suffer the entire squeeze.

3. *Political.* A family of difficulties which is neither upright nor downright, neither horizontal nor vertical, but consists of pressure, by particular groups, to allow their commodity prices to rise faster and further than the general level. Specifically, the important items here are farm products and labor.

4. *Geographical.* The fact that many a commodity costs more here where we consume it than out there where it was made, and that living standards and price levels have always differed in various parts of the country.

5. *Chronological.* The annoying discovery that conditions will not stay put and compel constant changes in price schedules.

6. *Tactical.* The multiple and unforeseeable evasions and violations which can be invented by ingenious men.

Each of these six difficulties can be illustrated by examples:

1. *Horizontal.* Perhaps because the "guns or butter" dilemma is now so familiar, Dr. Julius Hirsch's story about butter price-fixing in Germany during the First World War seems to be the classic demonstration of this difficulty. Anxious to protect the working man, the government fixed the price of butter, only to discover, in successive waves of dismay, that it had neglected to fix the prices of oleomargarine, of other cooking fats, and of rancid butter. The price of each of these products popped to disproportionate heights before the government caught up with them; and the price structure, even after the freezing action, was left badly deranged.

The real denouement came with an expedition back to the farm in order to discover why the supply of butter so greatly diminished in the face of these regulations. Only then was it recollected that no one had fixed the price of axle grease, and lubricants were very scarce in Germany at that time. Farmers, being practical fellows, had found butter a very satisfactory lubricant, especially when one must sell several pounds of butter to buy one pound of axle grease, or risk severe punishment by secret sale of butter above the fixed price.

The O.P.A. in this country has been careful to avoid horizontal price fixing difficulties wherever possible. For instance, on June 27th, 1941, an announcement was issued that the price of cottonseed oil was being investigated and measures would be taken to prevent successive price increases. However, nothing happened until August 29th when regulations were issued "to eliminate speculative and inflationary price practices" in fats and oils and their products, but included no specific price fixing. The administrator at that time pointed out that 1,800 edible fats and oils are sold on our market and a price ceiling on cottonseed oil "that did not extend to competitive fats and oils would be unwise and discriminatory."

On a smaller scale, the horizontal difficulty is encountered between grades of the same product. The price schedule issued by O.P.A. on scrap iron and steel covered 25 grades instead of the one "low-grade" usually alleged by the junk man who comes to buy your scrap.

2. *Vertical.* The vertical difficulties of price fixing can be scanned from either the top or the bottom end. In Canada and Germany price fixing started with the retailer; but the retailer finds it hard to sell at the fixed price, if he cannot also buy at a fixed price. Manufacturers and wholesalers quickly squeeze his margin to the vanishing point, or if his margin is also fixed, the manufacturer may be squeezed between a fixed price and an increasing labor cost. Conversely, if the process is started at the manufacturing end, as was attempted in this country, the producer may be in a straightjacket, but the profiteering retailer may still be free to squeeze the consumer. Price fixing at the manufacturing stage really holds the umbrella only over government

purchases and it may leave the consumer to shift mainly for himself.

Margin control appears to be the partial solution; but no panacea will remove all the difficulties. This concept is that no manufacturer shall add to the cost of his materials any more than the ordinary margin to cover manufacturing operations, and distributors likewise shall confine themselves to the usual margin. This does not guarantee a stationary price, but may prevent a runaway. This procedure in itself, of course, has the difficulty that the average retailer's accounting and knowledge of margin percentages is often not sound, and, secondly, that margins vary according to size of store, size of town and other factors. In any case, margin control, applied with care and vigilance seems well worth the effort, particularly because it places the burden on the seller's soul and probably on the seller's lawyer, rather than on the shoulders of a government bureau.

As yet little vertical price fixing has been done in this country. The only examples are in the field of iron and steel, where informal agreements or formal price orders govern prices all the way from pig iron down to some specific steel products; also in the case of cotton where government action, through subsidy or price order, controls the price from the bale through the combed yarn to grey goods.

Any attempt at vertical price control raises many an unsolved problem. For instance, it might seem possible to fix the price of soap at every stage from the manufacturer to the consumer. It is a staple and relatively standard product subject to chemical analysis, but how can the retail price be fixed by the cake when the public continues to desire and obtain a myriad of sizes, wrappings and perfumes? In the field of women's clothing, direct price fixing is almost hopeless, both because of rapidly changing styles and because of the "price line" theory of merchandising widely followed in the business. The retail price of a popular line of goods may remain the same for years on end with variations of cost absorbed by variations in quality of the product.

3. *Political.* The most serious political difficulty is the pressure of the farm bloc demanding that the farmer's relative position in the price structure be improved; that his standard of living go up at a time when war production makes inevitable a decline in the standard of living of the country as a whole.

The labor problem is similar, but probably less crucial. Immediate labor, that is labor expended directly in the manufacturing process, constitutes almost one-half of the cost of manufacturing. So price fixing looks, at first glance, hopeless without control of this half. At the same time Congressmen from labor districts appear to constitute more than one-half of the House of Representatives, which adds to the hopelessness. It is just as difficult for organized labor to see the country's total problem as it is for the farmer.

The hopeful side is that if other prices can be held down labor will have less basis for demanding increases on account of increased costs of living. In any case, Mr. Henderson's hesitancy to undertake wage regulation seems to me entirely sensible. He suggests that if wage regulation must be undertaken, a separate organization should be entrusted with it.

4. *Geographical.* Unless one is willing to undertake at a single stroke the reform of all inequities in our present social structure and a defiance of the cost of transportation, it will not do to impose a single uniform price structure on the entire country. For instance, it has long been known that wages are lower in the Southern part of the country because price levels have been lower and standards of living, regrettably, have been lower.

Perhaps further study should be given to that problem some day, but even the ardent reformers are now, I believe, overwhelmingly devoted to the immediate project of winning the war. Consequently, they are taking existing regional differentials into account. Other regional differences in prices are matters of economic geography and physical science. It will cost more to grow oranges in a hothouse in New York than outdoors in

Florida or California. Steel products will always cost more at a distance from sources of iron ore, limestone and fuel than they do at Pittsburgh or other major field centers; whether the cost is measured in "Pittsburgh plus" prices or in human effort. I believe these natural causes account for the fact that prices of food are low while manufactured goods are generally high on the Pacific Coast.

For instance, the O.P.A. price order governing sale of scrap steel provided prices in 13 different districts. Much more detail will probably be necessary in controlling the prices of some types of consumer goods, whereas other types of consumer goods are nationally advertised and sold at one uniform price through the entire country or a large portion of it.

The solution of this difficulty apparently consists of careful study of these geographical differences, though in some cases, the delay for complete study might be more harmful to the country than a few mistakes resulting from haste. Particularly important are the local boards or cooperating bodies which have been found necessary in every country where price fixing has been attempted. The problem yet to be solved is the relative amount of discretion to be allowed these local bodies with respect to specific prices.

5. *Chronological.* It seems that a new shortage develops almost every minute in Washington. The O.P.A. has found new price action needed with increasing frequency. For instance, take the 12-month period, ending February 1, 1942. In the first three months, six price orders were issued; in the next three months, six orders; in the third three months, 26 orders; in the fourth three months, 37 orders.

Not only is there constant need for attack in new sectors of the price campaign, but no one part of the problem apparently wants to stay licked. For instance, the iron and steel scrap price order was amended 11 times in the period from April 3 to date. Aluminum scrap prices have been amended five times since March 24; cotton grey goods six times since June 27. Several other schedules have been amended more than twice. The changes are usually upward to prevent the disappearance of the scarce items from the market and keep them in line with the general rise in level of prices.

Just a week or so ago, you probably noted further changes in copper, lead and zinc prices, where the general ceiling level has been raised in order to bring out additional production while bonuses are offered for additional production over and above the level of last year.

It is quite possible for price ceilings to restrict the supply of any given commodity in a dangerous degree. The first price order placed on cotton grey goods practically abolished trading in the textile lines in New York City until an amendment broke the deadlock.

There is no general solution for this type of problem. The solution so far discovered consists in part of propaganda and in part of compromise of the divergent factors.

6. *Tactical.* Throughout history criminals have found ways of evading the law and escaping jail. Human ingenuity found ways to evade the minimum prices ordered during N.R.A. and will now again probably strain our enforcement machinery. The advantage at present is that patriotic feeling is strong.

All of you are familiar with the ingenious evasions of minimum prices which were devised by buyers and sellers during the N.R.A. Many of you have heard Dr. Julius Hirsch's story of cattle sales under a fixed price ceiling in Germany following the First World War. The cattle were conscientiously sold at the required price, but an alleged surplus of dogs made it necessary to sell a dog with each two head of cattle. That this dog was a well-trained animal was evident from the substantial price he commanded; and it became further evident by the fact that he always found his way back to his original master within a day or two.

Secret markets of rationed and price-fixed goods have been giving trouble even in well-disciplined England. It will need all of the traditional sense of responsibility and patriotic loyalty which we believe we possess in this country to prevent the same ugly developments here.

The solution here again is hard work, foresight, a willingness to learn from the experiences of other countries and ingenuity to match the ingenuity of the minority of citizens, christened "the chiselers." Above all it is necessary to cultivate and sustain public and local interest in the enforcement problem.

PRICE FIXING AND COMMODITY CONTROL [5]

I want to say something about the philosophy of the bill first. The great function of price control in a war is to conserve scarce commodities needed for war, and scarce necessities of life for the people, and to make sure that they are better distributed and better allocated for war purposes and for the life and health of the people than they would be if left to the play of the open markets.

Scarce necessities of life and scarce things needed for war: When the problem is put in those terms there is a definite philosophy and a manageable problem. There is a recognition that you have got to connect your priorities, your rationing, and your allocations very definitely with price fixing. There is a holding back in price-fixing edict to what can be administered.

But we have a different philosophy behind this price-fixing bill. We are told by Mr. Henderson, for example—and I quote him exactly:

> I think that one of the most acute necessities in price regulation is the necessity for having a low price level for the future.

That is from the unrevised hearings before the House Committee, page 343.

[5] By Benjamin M. Anderson, Professor of Economics, University of California at Los Angeles; Consulting Economist, Capital Research Company. Testimony before the Senate Committee on Banking and Currency on the Price-Control Bill, December 16, 1941. *Economic Bulletin.* 3:3-14. December 16, 1941.

PERMANENT PRICE CONTROL POLICY

We are told again and again by Mr. Henderson that the relaxing of price control after the war was over—after the last war was over—allowed a 40 to 50 per cent rise in commodity prices and that, therefore, the price control should not be limited in time, but should be left to the discretion of the President, so that a postwar slump may be avoided.

Now, parenthetically, Mr. Henderson is quite wrong in saying that there was a 40 to 50 per cent increase in commodity prices after the war. On the 1913 base, prices rose to 207 at the peak of the war; and then at the peak of the postwar boom, in May of 1920, they went to 248. That is a 20 per cent increase, not a 40 to 50 per cent increase. That is the old series of Bureau of Labor Statistics number. The new series on the 1926 basis, with more commodities in it, shows approximately the same postwar rise, about 21 per cent.

Congress must make a very sharp determination as to whether its purpose in providing a price-fixing bill is to meet the practical exigencies of scarce essentials during the war, or whether its purpose is to create a vast machine for postwar governmental economic planning. I emphatically do not believe that price fixing should last after the war. Having in mind that in the last war legislation designed to end when the war ended did not end then because there was a long delay in getting the peace treaty ratified, I would want to draw the terms very definitely as to the time. I think you would do very well to pass your bill for one year, and then let them come back to you in a year, telling you what they are doing as they ask for renewal of the authority. You will give them renewal of authority if the war is still on; but if they are not doing it right, you will restrict their powers, and the fact that they will have to come back to you will be the greatest safeguard against the abuse of power. I would limit it to one year....

I do not believe it should be the function of the present price-fixing legislation to meet a postwar economic readjustment. I agree that it is undesirable that we should have a great slump in commodity prices after the war. I agree that an unnecessary rise in commodity prices during the war would mean an unnecessarily drastic price readjustment after the war. But I do not believe that a decline in prices following the war need involve any unmanageable economic consequences.

There was a 30 per cent fall in prices in the Northern states when the Civil War was over. That was a decline that everybody expected and a decline that did no harm. People expected it and were braced for it. The South suffered very greatly after the Civil War, but the North went on in its stride. It had no real economic trouble until 1873, and that was not due to a postwar slump in commodity prices. You will find the background of this in Wesley Mitchell's *History of the Greenbacks*.

Our break in commodity prices from 248 on the 1913 base in May 1920 to 141 in August of 1921 was a very drastic and severe thing. I lived through that thing with a great bank, watching the economic consequences, helping to place loans where they would do the most good, studying the effects on many industries. Our contacts from out the Chase Bank ran out over the country. . . .

If that break had come in 1918, after the armistice, when it was generally expected, it would have done very little harm. We were braced for it. The delay of two years made it a much more severe thing. But the reaction to that great break in commodity prices was amazingly slight. We had what we thought then was terrific unemployment in the summer of 1921. We had 6,000,000 men unemployed. We had a great many business failures. Net corporate deficits for the year were $2,685,000,000, taking profits and losses together.

But we had no government interference with the readjustment. We made it quickly. The tide turned in August 1921, and, gentlemen, we had a labor shortage in the spring of 1923. The government left it to the people to work out. The government, old-fashioned, considered its business to be the protection of the solvency of the Treasury. It cut expenses. It released men from the Army, the Navy, and the civil service. It cut expenses, and it cut taxes, though not quite so much. It overbalanced the budget every year. In the worst panic year it pared down the public debt $300,000,000. Old-fashioned? It didn't know any better; it didn't know anything about this new economic wisdom. It let the people alone.

SENATOR TOBEY. Do you have your fingers crossed when you say "wisdom"?

DR. ANDERSON. That was meant sarcastically. . . .

I do not want a governmental agency created by this legislation that is going to try to manage us when that postwar period comes. There is not the wisdom to do it. The best economists could not do it. The Administration cannot do it. The people have got to work it out.

If we compare the 6,000,000 of unemployed that we had in the summer of 1921 with the much larger unemployment for the much longer period, 1933-39, of governmental economic planning, I think we can see that there are some things worse than what we went through in 1921.

I do not think that Congress should vote a price-fixing bill the purpose of which is to control postwar prices. I think that Congress should recognize that the main control of the general price level is not to be found in a price-fixing bill but rather in the adoption of other measures, including a sound Treasury borrowing policy, a sound monetary policy, a sound taxation policy, and a sound labor policy. I heard just a bit of Mr. Hoover's statement this morning. I think he emphasized the same point very strongly—the connection between price fixing, on the one hand, and priority allocations and rationing, on the other hand, with the contention that they should be in the hands of the same body. I would emphatically urge that upon you.

In the hearings before the House Committee there was recognition on the part of the witnesses, among them Chairman Eccles, Mr. Donald Nelson, and Mr. Henderson, that there is a close connection between price fixing and priorities.

Mr. Nelson would restrict priorities and price fixing to scarce things.

Chairman Eccles says:

> I see no good reason for attempting the impossible task . . . of undertaking to police not merely those prices which need to be policed because of scarcity but all prices.

Yet this bill as drawn has nothing to say about scarcity or about priorities. It is a price-fixing bill. The reason, presumably, is that authority for priorities and allocations is contained in other legislation; but there is no connection made in the law between the two. There is no congressional policy stated linking the two. There is nothing in any legislation connecting the two in such a way as to require that the authorities connected with price fixing and the authorities connected with priorities shall even confer with one another.

In the last war we had the closest connection between the two. No one general authority fixed prices, and no one general authority gave allocations or gave priorities. Rather we had a Food Administration which took control of scarce foods, allocated and rationed them, and fixed their prices to the extent that price fixing was done.

We had a Fuel Administration which, again, not only fixed prices but also took control of supplies. We undertook to do a very practical job in the last war, unhampered by a multitude of conflicting theories. . . .

You ought to define your policy very clearly here. Are we to attempt by a general price-fixing bill a general control of all prices and of all the commodity price levels? Or are we to limit ourselves to the problem of managing, commodity by commodity, those commodities which by virtue of scarcity and essential character need to be conserved under the pressure of war needs? The latter is a manageable problem; the former is an undertaking far too ambitious for any price-fixing administration to undertake. We can do a great deal about the general price level, the level of all prices, but not by direct price fixing and certainly not by price fixing which is not linked with allocations, priorities, and rationing. The holding down of the general price level must be by a variety of indirect measures, which include the taxing and borrowing policy of the government, the removal of interferences with production, notably the 40-hour-week law, and the reversal of the policy of cheap money.

Free prices have work to do. Free prices have the important function of accomplishing priorities, allocations, and rationing. That is what they do; that is their regular work. It is the work of free prices and freely moving wages to determine whether labor and supplies shall be drawn to the production of commodity A or commodity B—rising prices, more production; falling prices, less production. Rising prices, less consumption; falling prices, more consumption. That is the work prices do. It is their business to see, with freely moving prices, that the commodities produced shall be divided up among consumers in accordance with the relative urgencies of demand. When prices are fixed something has got to be done to do the work that the prices would otherwise do. You have got to allocate, give priorities, ration.

If the government holds down the price and does nothing more, the production of the commodity affected will be restricted, and the demand for it will be greater than would be the case at higher prices. The supply will be much more rapidly depleted than would otherwise be the case. To meet this, the government must take further steps, amounting in extreme cases even to the drafting of labor and resources.

Price fixing by itself tends to derange perversely the control of production and consumption. It restricts production. Price fixing must not be undertaken without these other things.

It follows from this that price fixing ought not to be pushed in advance of the development of machinery for commodity control; and it follows, I think, that it ought to be very definitely limited to scarce things needed either for war or else necessities of life for the civilian population. . . .

In the last war we moved with vigor and decision in controlling essentials. But we made no effort to fix the prices of nonessentials and no effort to fix the prices of luxuries. We limited their production, but we allowed their prices to rise, and we allowed the rising prices to restrict their consumption.

In the case of scarce necessities of life, we fixed the price, and we made strenuous efforts to ration. I won't say anything about sugar, in the interest of saving time. It is discussed in the 1917 address which I am offering for your record.

I do not think there is any justification for the price fixing of nonessentials. I think it is fantastic. . . .

A further point is that if you are going to deal with a wide range of commodities and undertake to do it with justice and undertake to do it on sound economic lines and take control of supply, you are going to have an administrative machine created with needlessly many people in it at a wholly needless cost. That machine is going to be pretty big anyhow at best.

PRICE FIXING OF AGRICULTURAL PRODUCTS [6]

Any plan of price fixing should meet two general requirements. It must first be economically sound, that is there must be some real economic objective that can be brought about by the price fixing and that will be secured by it. Secondly, it must be administratively feasible. No plan, however desirable it may be from an economic viewpoint, is worth anything unless it can be administered. The difficulties of administration will be lessened to the extent to which the market can be made to function in its usual capacity during the period of price fixing. This suggests that whenever there is a choice of means for accomplish-

[6] By Warren C. Waite, Department of Agriculture, University of Minnesota. *American Statistical Association. Journal.* 37:13-21. March, 1942.

ing a desired result, the one that provides a larger degree of automatic regulation through the agencies now available should be employed. The price administrator should conceive of his function as that of assisting the market to operate in a way beneficial to the common purpose, rather than one of supplanting or replacing the normal market.

In order to fix prices on agricultural products it is necessary to have in view the underlying economic purposes of such price fixing. Two important but partly contradictory purposes stand out at once. The first is to aid in the allocation of the costs of the war among the various groups in the community and in the case of agricultural price fixing the allocation between agriculture and the other groups. The second is to guide agricultural production during the war with a view of securing adequate supplies and adjusting agriculture to a position to be able to withstand the shock of returning to a peacetime economy. Preventing agricultural prices from rising too high will aid in restraining a general rise in all prices in several ways. Lower agricultural prices will lessen the cost of purchase of many goods bought by the government. It will also keep the cost of food to workers lower, and this should lessen the pressure from the laboring classes for wage increases. Food is a large part of the worker's budget and a part in which he seems to be especially aware of price changes. Moreover, many persons will fail to secure appreciably higher incomes during the coming period, and for these persons a rise in food costs might create considerable hardships. Keeping agricultural prices down would also dampen the rise in agricultural incomes and lessen the increase in purchasing power in the hands of the farmer. This would curtail his ability to buy other goods and in consequence his contribution toward inflation. There is thus in setting agricultural prices an income allocation between agriculture and the remainder of the community. This includes the tacit assumption that income or purchasing power in other hands is more diffused, less influential in producing price rises, or more subject to control than when in the hands of the farmers.

Price fixing also offers an opportunity to adjust agriculture toward an allocation of resources deemed more desirable and to accomplish this without the high cost to the remainder of society that might be involved if all prices were allowed to remain free to rise. Allocation of resources among productive enterprises in agriculture depends a great deal upon the relative prices of products. It is only the total volume of resources utilized by agriculture that depends in large part upon the level of prices. Total agricultural resources are not going to change very greatly either under high or low levels of agricultural prices, but considerable shifts among enterprises will take place with changes in the relative prices of products. Expansion of total agricultural production is likely to be nearly as great with a fair increase in income as it would be with an enormous increase in income.

To say that we want to adjust agriculture is not, however, to say that we are entirely certain just what that adjustment should be. The immediate problem is fairly clear, but the long-run problem is extremely uncertain. Immediately we need a schedule of requirements for the war effort together with the requirements for emergency stocks. There should naturally be a schedule in terms of absolute minimums and another of desirable quantities. We also need to recognize that it is more desirable to err on the side of too much rather than too little. We can always use up too much even if the process is painful for many, but deficits might be fatal.

This is not, however, to say that we should close our eyes to the future following the war even if our present view of this future is vague. It is obvious that we must currently produce what is essential to the prosecution of the war, but we must also keep in view the long-run as far as we are able. It is essential that we do this because we cannot avoid the difficulties of the future by the simple assumption that any increase in production

PERMANENT PRICE CONTROL POLICY 43

induced now will be demanded by ourselves and our neighbors following the war. There may be needs from a nutritional viewpoint in our own population and from a humanitarian viewpoint for Europe, but whether a people in the crisis of a great adjustment to a peace economy and already burdened by the costs of a contribution to a war can freely give or will be willing to is an undecided question. The war, rather than solving our agricultural problem, will serve only to intensify it at the close, and present plans must keep an eye upon the possibilities of this future.

Any price fixed for agricultural products must face, perhaps in the law providing for price fixing and certainly among the farmers themselves, the handicap of comparison with "parity" prices. The idea or concept of parity is one which has come to be associated with the idea of right or justice in the minds of many agricultural leaders and the farmers themselves. Any ceiling set at parity levels would be likely to be accepted at once by the agricultural group as "fair," while it is conceivable that any price set below parity would be felt unjust if not actually objected to.

The idea of parity found its first legislative expression nearly a decade ago in the Agricultural Adjustment Act of 1933. In this Act it was declared to be the policy of Congress to reestablish prices to farmers at a level that would give agricultural commodities a purchasing power with respect to articles that farmers buy equivalent to the purchasing power of agricultural commodities in a base period. Briefly the essential calculation is to multiply the average price of the commodity in the base period, usually August 1909 to July 1914, by the index of the cost of things bought by the farmer, with the base of this latter index also from 1910 to 1914. This underlying idea has been expanded and developed in later agricultural legislation in various ways and has come to saturate agricultural proposals of many kinds.

Parity price and parity income have become an important ethical concept of what farmers ought to have in view of a situation in an earlier period. Price fixing in a war period should be unhampered by any legislative requirement to provide some historical relationship. The price administrators should be left free to operate as current conditions demand. The difficulty with parity prices as a criterion for ceilings in a war emergency is that they may be and probably are too high to provide the results selected as desirable or demanded in the fixing of many prices in such a period. In retrospect, the period 1910 to 1914 appears especially favorable for agricultural prices in relation to non-agricultural prices. To continue such a relationship in peacetimes is to invite the accumulation of forces tending to destroy this very relationship, and to force a set of price relationships of twenty-five years earlier on a price administrator is to handicap severely, if not to defeat completely, his efforts. Cost relationships among the commodities have changed greatly, and to provide parity prices for some commodities would perhaps stimulate their production greatly. To offset these shifts it would be necessary to establish price differences between prices to enable the ceilings to exercise a directive function and a requirement of parity for the lowest prices in such a system might easily lift the entire level so high as to lose all possible inflationary control. If parity prices as minimum requirements in themselves promise to be faulty, then all that can be said about the proposal to provide a 110 per cent of parity minimum for any ceiling established is to make nearly certain the failure of agricultural price controls. . . .

It is when we come to the field of production and the holding of commodities that price fixing may be expected to result in the greatest changes from the usual procedures of the market. To a large extent many of these changes will be unforseeable and unusual in their character. The decisions with respect to agricultural production are made by a multitude of farmers upon their individual farms. At certain times of the year, or perhaps in some cases less frequently, the farmer must canvass his resources and the prospects for returns in the future with a view of the best utilization of those resources. In this allocation prospective prices, naturally, occupy an important place in calculations under ordinary circumstances. With price uncertain there will be a wide variety of estimates as to the probable price and a variety of reactions to the same estimate on the part of different producers depending upon their faith in their own judgment and the inclination to take risks in the hopes of larger returns. With prices established, many of these uncertainties vanish and the calculations of what will be profitable differ materially. We will probably be wrong if we base our assumption of responses on historical relationships and do not modify them by some sort of an adjustment for this difference. This pre-supposes that prices are announced in advance, and such an announcement would be essential if prices are to exercise a directive force over agricultural production.

There are additional difficulties in establishing the prices of agricultural products beyond determining the level for them in a particular period. These arise because of the seasonal character of production and the variation in the volume of production in various years. Many agricultural products have wide seasonal movements in their prices. These are induced by the heavy production at certain periods of the year and the necessity of storage to level out the rate of movement into consumption and for the processing of the product. It is evident that the price fixed will need to include a seasonal movement. This seasonal must be reasonably correct, otherwise great peculiarities in the rate of marketing may take place. If a single price is established for the year, then there will be no incentive to hold and everything will tend to go to the market at once unless some sort of a quota system is established for sales. Some system of monthly quotas for sellers could of course be devised, but such an administrative task would be an unwarranted undertaking in view of more important requirements for administration elsewhere. If, however, a very large seasonal advance is provided in the established price, this would lead to holding for a later period and a scarcity in the market during the early period. The choice of the seasonal must lie in the experience of the past, and some average seasonal derived from recent years will probably prove satisfactory. It is also probable that there would be an advantage in lessening the rise in the seasonal price somewhat below the average with a view of erring on the side of increasing the rate of early marketing rather than retarding it. This would insure the marketing agencies receiving the products at the full rate at which they could be adequately handled, and if only a slight price decline below the established ceiling were induced in the early period, the expected higher later price would tend to balance marketings to the more usual previous rates.

Problems are also raised by the necessity of carryovers from one year to the next. For some products these carryovers are fairly large. The carryover tends to increase when the following crop promises to be small and prices high, and the carryover declines in years when the following crop promises to be large and prices low. The price set or expected for the subsequent year will in consequence have a great deal to do with the extent of carryover during the given year. If the price set for the new crop is materially higher one would of course immediately decide to hold to the later period. Where units of new and old production are distinguishable it may be possible to establish differential prices for them to prevail in the later period. It is possible that usual marketing rates and timing may be considerably upset by failure to gauge this factor. The new situation with ceilings will differ greatly from the old where prices were free to fluctuate. Without ceilings the outlook with respect to price in the future is uncertain, and holdovers of products may offer considerable advantages even though it appears on current information that prices will be lower in the new year. It is always possible that something will happen to greatly decrease supplies or increase demand at the last moment. Thus a small probable loss is balanced against a great possible gain if the unexpected does happen. Removal of this possibility must necessarily exercise a decided influence upon the propensity of operators to store. Instead of uncertainty and a reward for good judgment, the storage decision now becomes largely established by the price fixing. Storage either would or would not be profitable. In such a situation it may be necessary and indeed probably will be necessary for the government to enter into the holding of products on a considerable scale and stand ready to buy or dispose of products at the established price.

This review of the problems of agricultural price fixing makes it evident that no predetermined single method will be adequate to do the job required. We cannot afford to freeze agricultural prices at any given level or in any relationship now prevailing. Furthermore, greater flexibility is required than would be obtained by tying prices to parity at any predetermined level.

Agriculture is a vast industry with many ramifications, and the price fixing must be simple and direct unless it is to become completely unwieldy and too complex for administration. The general policy must be one of utilizing the usual regulative forces of the economy to the fullest extent possible. This means that the price fixing authority must be conversant with industry and its markets and be prepared to assist the market to carry out its functions rather than to slap on a fixed set of controls. Fortunately in the accumulated knowledge and experience of the workers in agriculture, particularly in the Department of Agriculture, there is a vast reservoir to be drawn upon, and we may confidently look forward to any legislatively unhampered experiment in price fixing in agricultural products to be carried through with a considerable prospect of success.

THE CONSEQUENCES OF INFLATION [7]

The consequences of inflation are the consequences of the stage which it is permitted to reach. We have already passed

[7] From article "Statement of Considerations Involved in the Issuance of the General Maximum Price Regulation." *Federal Reserve Bulletin.* 28:442-4 May, 1942.

through a mild stage of inflationary price advance. We are entering . . . a more severe and extensive stage—a stage where the upward movement of prices will increase both in magnitude and in tempo. Beyond that stage lies the fatal spiral which engulfed the countries of Central Europe following the First World War.

The first stage, that which we have already experienced, is itself a warning of what is to come. Many of our people with smaller incomes have already seen the necessaries of life pass beyond the reach of their slender means. They have already experienced the sense of hopelessness and frustration which comes with the change from subsistence to a deeper poverty. They have already brought their children to a table from which accustomed and necessary foods have been removed by rising prices.

Suspicion of undue advantage and profiteering has already been engendered between farmer and worker, and worker and employer. True unity of purpose must rest on the conviction that reward and sacrifice are received and rendered in common. The irregular, uncertain, and manipulative advances in prices which characterize all stages of inflation have already damaged that conviction.

In a narrower sense, inflation has already multiplied the cost of the war. The price rises which have occurred since September 1939 will increase by 35 billions of dollars the money cost of the war program now authorized. The total cost of the First World War, by comparison was 31 billions, and that 31 billions, it is estimated, included 13½ billions of inflated prices.

These things have already happened. They are behind us. The next stage of inflation—the one that we now face—will extend this pattern. And it will add to it a new and far more serious configuration. If unchecked, inflation will launch a race between the wages of the stronger bargaining groups and the cost of living. This means constant revision of wage contracts, constant bargaining and negotiation, and the certain prospect of interrupted production. The normal collective bargaining processes are strained, perhaps broken. Business commitments are placed on a month-to-month, perhaps on a week-to-week basis. Business planning gives way to make-shift decision. War production is shackled and perhaps disrupted. It may be paralyzed.

In a sense, inflation is a substitute for production. Money is made not by producing commodities, but by withholding them from use. Scarce materials find their way into inventories and hoards, and profit is derived from advancing markets. The speculator rather than the producer becomes the successful businessman. Materials that might yield tanks and guns for the armed forces, or food and clothing for our people at home, are surreptitiously routed to the warehouse.

Those whose incomes are small and fixed have already suffered. During the stage of inflation now ahead, their position will become desperate. The well-stocked store will become an empty fraud for our old people who live on annuities and pensions, for dependents of our soldiers and sailors, and for the substandard wage groups whose bargaining position is weak. The prices of necessaries will have passed beyond their reach. For during inflation goods are reserved for the person with the longest pocketbook, the person who is able to protect himself during the upward spiral, or the person who has turned the spiral to his selfish advantage.

The pattern of disaster which attends the final stage of inflation is well known. In this stage prices are revised upward weekly and then daily. Incomes enter into a crazy race with prices. Money is something to be passed on as quickly as possible. It is no longer a symbol of stability but a mark of social disintegration. Thrift and saving become incompatible with self-preservation. Savings, investments, life insurance policies, all the results of past thrift, become worthless. Legitimate business disappears; speculation and profiteering remain. Organized government itself is undermined.

The hopelessness and frustration of the early stages of inflation soon turn to anger and despair.

To think of mobilization of resources for war in such an environment is the merest fancy.

Inflation does not always run its full course, although between the present stage and the final collapse there is no definite stopping place. But the principle can be laid down that the greater the period over which the process extends without complete and effective control, the more serious and painful is the task of stopping it, and the more dangerous the demoralization which must follow. The present inflationary movement may, of course, end, not with wild inflation, but with the end of the war and war-occasioned spending. Or it might be brought to a halt by measures such as those which are now being taken. In the first case, the clear consequence would be a complete and ruinous deflation. Those who were not destroyed by the inflation would be ruined by the ensuing collapse. And deflation, even more than inflation, has shown itself the cause of social disorganization. It was more than a decade after the First World War before agriculture and much of labor and industry in the United States recovered from the wreckage of the 1921 collapse. More serious still, there were wrecked lives and disbanded families for whom there was no recovery at all.

Inflation might also be checked sometime in the future by measures such as those now being taken. Of this it is necessary to say but one thing. While the present measures are painful, they are far less painful than those that would be required a year hence. It is never easy to check an inflationary movement. But there will never be a time when it will be less painful than now.

AMERICA IN REVOLUTION [8]

About a year ago a professor of philosophy in New York University wrote a book whose importance is only now beginning

[8] Editorial. *Christian Century.* 59:623-5. May 13, 1942.

to be recognized. Professor Burnham called his book *The Managerial Revolution*. When it first appeared he was accused of preaching fascism, socialism, or at the very least collectivism in some form. Mr. Burnham replied that he was not preaching anything; he was simply trying to describe the process by which the control of government and society is changing in the contemporary world. This change, he declared, consists of the passing of power into the hands of the "managers." These men are not owners; they are not financiers; they are managers. It would be hard to find a better illustration of Mr. Burnham's thesis than has now been supplied by Mr. Henderson. The scene which took place in that Washington room the afternoon Mr. Henderson announced his price regulations marked a new high point in America's own "managerial revolution."

Here and there individuals are trying to convince themselves that all that is happening in the United States today is merely the adoption of a series of temporary measures to meet a war emergency. Let the emergency pass, let peace be declared, and they predict that the nation will drop back into the capitalistic patterns which it has followed from its birth. But is this just a war emergency program, destined to pass with the war? Last summer Philip D. Reed said: "Our political, social and economic scheme of things after the war will resemble neither the 1920's nor the 1930's. The war will advance by several decades the trends away from laissez faire and toward economic planning under government supervision." The man who said that is neither a New Dealer nor a socialistic soapboxer. He is the chairman of the board of the General Electric Company. Most of Mr. Reed's associates in the higher realms of big business agree with him. They may curse such a prospect, but they recognize its reality.

The fact is that it is now generally acknowledged that a postwar collapse of the American economy can be prevented only by an indefinite continuation of the various measures for government planning and control which are now being taken to deal with the war emergency. Consider, for example, the single factor of manpower after the war. The National Resources Planning Board has shown that if the war should continue until 1944 and stop then, there would be at least 27,000,000 men released from the army and from war industries who, unless they could be absorbed in an economy kept producing at maximum levels, would precipitate not simply an economic depression but a complete collapse. In some way those 27,000,000 men must be absorbed in productive industry. Only a government planned economy can cope with such a problem.

More important, the American people have glimpsed the possibilities of an economy of abundance in this war emergency. The dogmas of finance no longer persuade them. They know that when a community, a nation, has sufficient materials and sufficient manpower it can produce on a hitherto undreamed-of scale without worrying about debt or interest rates or returns on investment. And they reason that if a nation can thus be kept producing in maximum volume in time of war, it can do the same thing in time of peace. It can do so, they are beginning to understand, by allowing the government to exercise the same powers of control and planning which it exercises in wartime. Moreover, they are also beginning to reflect on the significance of the prospect that, after the war, their dealings must be with other nations which, in one form or another, will be under planned economies.

Stuart Chase, in his new book, *The Road We Are Traveling*, has summed up this situation with characteristic eloquence: "If you hold your ear close to the ground, you can hear a muffled roar echoing around the whole world. It does not come from bombs, or thunder on the Russian front. It is the voice of the people demanding security and an end to the paradox of plenty. It is the revolt of the masses asking for the food which farmers let rot upon the ground or dump into the streams. This subterranean roar is the most powerful force in the world today. Statesmen who listen to it will be upheld. Statesmen who shut their ears will be buried, no matter how lofty their sentiments about freedom and initiative."

He continues,

> Science and invention have put an adequate standard of living within the reach of every family in the great industrial nations. Ultimately it will be within the reach of every family in the world. The mass of the people know this. Yet the standard of living which they might have does not come through to the majority of them. Why does it not come through? It is there for all to see—13,000,000 bales of cotton in storage, 500,000,000 bushels of wheat in granaries in the United States, 60,000,000 bags of coffee burned in Brazil—why does it not come through? The authorities reply that the market cannot tolerate it, or that the laws of property forbid it. Do you think these answers, however legal and logical, are going to satisfy the masses? They are asking a revolutionary question which demands a revolutionary answer.

The war has only hastened the revolution which Mr. Henderson's price fixing and rent freezing order typified. If the Republicans, or any other political party, try to reverse this process they will be annihilated. The nation cannot turn back history's clock; it cannot return along this road on which its feet have been set. It has entered upon a revolution, and no man today can see the end. We know only one thing assuredly, that the old order has been left behind. It is gone—that order of "rugged" individualism, of free enterprise (which has been a long way from free for most of us). It is dead—that world dominantly controlled by the profit motive. That is something to ponder in this year when a forward-looking church conference held the profit motive too potent a shibboleth to be repudiated by name.

But if the old order has been left behind, what is to come? Many minds are working on that question; many voices are trying to answer it. A report issued this month by the Twentieth Century Fund, entitled *Postwar Planning in the United States,* tells of more than a hundred agencies which are now at work on the requirements of a planned economy for America. Among these are thirty-five bureaus or commissions in departments of the government. The proposals which such bodies make will vary widely, but all will agree in this—that the government is to have dominant power over the whole range of economic life in the postwar nation. Some see the government as the banker, the administrator, the engineer, the employer, the doctor, the teacher, the shipper, the exporter, the importer and perhaps even the undertaker. Others are trying to set theoretical limits at which government control in a planned society shall stop. These tend to believe that if the government is financier its grip on the community will be sufficient. All, however, see ahead a government "planned" society.

It is not necessary for the purposes of this editorial that the details of such a planned America should be discussed now. What is important is that it shall be recognized that this revolution is full upon us. "Planning" is no longer some future possibility for social and political theorists to talk about. It is *here.* The war emergency has brought it, and it will never pass, unless the nation elects to plunge into chaos. It is that, in truth, which has brought it—the belief that the nation's fate has narrowed down to a choice between planning or chaos.

But this, it may be objected, is not the America of the Founding Fathers. No, it is not. Their ideal was a state whose citizens experienced the absolute minimum of centralized control—a government of delegated powers, jealously limited. Now the citizen must delegate to the state the power to secure for himself work, food, shelter, security in old age and defense against foreign foes. The America which will emerge from this process may not be scarred with the marks of fighting at the barricades, but it will no more be the America of the first 125 years of the republic than the U.S.S.R. is the Russia of the tsars. The revolution is here; there can be no turning back. Does the Christian church realize this?

EFFECTS OF THE WAR ON PRICE POLICIES [9]

Price making and price policy during the postwar period will depend not only upon the competitive structure of industry (i.e., the number and relative importance of individual firms in different markets), and the willingness of firms to compete within that structure, but will depend also upon the extent to which government in the aftermath continues directly to control commodity prices.

This is partially a question of whether wartime price control will tend to perpetuate itself. Partially, also it is a question of the extent to which wartime influences, including price control, will have produced structural changes which, as reflected in the competitive structure of industry and the willingness of firms to compete therein, will make it more difficult to abandon price control.

There is doubtless a tendency for any control measure to give rise to a situation in which control seems to perpetuate itself. Illustrations of this tendency are numerous and we may cite as one the regulation of railroad rates which has become so entrenched in the American political and economic scene that its discontinuance is difficult to imagine. If we may use the phrase self-perpetuation of control, its general connotation is certainly that a control policy, once established, tends to bring into play forces which operate to prevent or to discourage its discontinuance. First, there is the influence of inertia, by which is meant that what exists tends to endure merely because forces of social inertia resist factors working for institutional change. Second, there is the vested interest of whatever bureaucracy develops to administer control.

The influence of inertia and of vested interests may be commented upon together. Viewed historically, each of these factors

[9] By John D. Sumner, University of Buffalo; Member of Staff, Office of Price Administration. *American Economic Review*. 32:Supplement 412-15. March, 1942.

would seem to have comparatively little influence in the perpetuation of those direct commodity price controls which developed during wartime. During the first World War this and every other important country in the conflict established direct price control; after that war price control was generally abandoned in rather short order. Public and governmental opinion, rather than regarding such control as a device or policy arising in the ordinary course of events, tended rather to regard price control as one among many necessary evils which should be endured only temporarily. Perhaps people will feel differently after this war, but one suspects that while no political leader may ever again say "back to normalcy," the American people will generally wish to put aside as many as possible of those unpleasantnesses which in their minds are associated directly with war. The majority of people in Washington today, as was true twenty years ago, wish to get the job over with and to return whence they came.

The most important forces operating to continue price control are not likely to be the influence of social inertia or vested interest, but rather the economic consequences of price control and other wartime developments, and their repercussions in the postwar period. If price control, for example, is so administered during war as significantly to reduce the number of firms, to increase the relative importance in the market of a few large enterprises, or to reduce the willingness of firms to compete within the structure of industry, then a situation will have been created in which it may be difficult to discontinue the regulation of prices. The same may also be said of the influence of priority controls and allocation policies upon postwar price regulation.

It is much too soon to predict the results in this direction. In discussing the influence of the war upon the competitive structure of industry and the willingness of firms to compete therein, I have earlier touched upon the issues which seem to me to be the most crucial to the central problem. Price and other controls per se need not affect the competitive structure of industry, the willingness of firms to compete, or otherwise lead to the continuance of price regulation. However, they may exert a significant albeit indirect effect upon postwar price control if, through the use of certain criteria, the number of firms is reduced or other aspects of the competitive situation are affected to a degree greater than that inherent in the underlying scarcity situation created by war.

Thus far, this paper has been restricted to a few suggestions with respect to the way in which such wartime influences as price control, resource reallocation, technological change, and the flux in ideas may operate to affect price making and policy in the immediate postwar period.

The net balance of conflicting influences at work in these areas and the extent to which their results continue in a period beyond the few years of immediate postwar readjustment is certainly a question that is too difficult to forecast. As is so often the case in discussions of this type, one takes refuge in the statement that "it all depends" on certain factors.

Among the relevant factors there are two of obvious but perhaps crucial importance. They are simply the extent to which the American economy is able to avoid severe and prolonged depression and, second, the extent to which American opinion is able to differentiate between two basically different types of control. If our economy faces prolonged and severe depression soon after the close of the war, few men would disagree to the proposition that the secular drift toward increasing control of our economy will rapidly accelerate. Whether a more collectivist pasture beyond the fence is really a greener pasture is a question about which everyone, including economists, will hold strong opinions. But there are few, I believe, who would dispute the proposition that the social and economic distress attendant upon a severe and prolonged depression following this war will make people want to see whether the pasture over the fence may not in fact be greener than the parched one in which they find themselves.

A prolonged and severe depression is certainly not an inevitable consequence of the present war. Whether we have such a depression will depend somewhat upon international circumstances partially outside our control; in part, however, the answer will depend upon how effectively this and other nations are able to stabilize, or place a floor under, the level of economic activity. In this task there will be many aids arising in part from the war itself. Among those which have been mentioned are the investment opportunities following from technological change, the need for industrial rehabilitation, and the power of demands pent up during the war period. Perhaps an even more powerful influence will flow from the existence, for a considerable period at least, of large potential markets outside our borders in both the new and old worlds.

If we are able, with the aid of such influences, reasonably to stabilize economic conditions after the war, price making and policy may, in fact, become more competitive than in years gone by. Here much will depend upon the flux in men's ideas, mentioned but not discussed earlier in this paper. Despite certain dissents, the achievement of economic stability at a comparatively high level of national income will generally not be aided by widespread price controls of either the maximum or the minimum variety. The direct control of certain commodity prices, while in some instances benefiting the industry involved, tends commonly to increase the burdens of adjustment elsewhere in the economy. Exceptions may be found, but in general, the proposition that the relative stability created in one area by minimum price control will operate to promote the cyclical stability of the whole economy is but another illustration of what has been termed elsewhere a "fallacy of composition."

The role of government in economic life may greatly increase at the same time that direct price controls are curtailed. Public investment in many noncompetitive areas, the major expansion of a social security system, and more complete and refined control of our credit structure—these and other types of

PERMANENT PRICE CONTROL POLICY 59

government policy may provide a powerful contribution toward economic stability. If they are successful, it will be possible for the price-making process as such to become an increasingly individualistic and competitive one.

Thus, more government control does not necessarily mean more price control. If in this country we come more clearly to recognize the difference between the consequences of the direct control of the price decisions of the market place, and government measures directed at minimizing the severity of depressions, price making and price policy may continue to be of a character compatible with an essentially individualistic economy. If, on the other hand, people continue indiscriminately to demand that the government "do something," this country, if it escapes severe and prolonged depression, is apt to do so by accident rather than by purposeful intent. If we do not escape such a depression, one may entertain the gravest doubts as to whether we will not at last have come to the often predicted end of competitive capitalism.

PROPOSED ORGANIZATION FOR PREVENTION OF UNJUSTIFIED PRICE INCREASES [10]

One thing stands out as a result of these hearings which should be accepted as a political fact. It is that the American people believe in a competitive system based on maximum opportunity for free enterprise, and that they think such a system can be maintained under present laws without fundamental change. They demand an organization which can make present laws effective. Therefore, I propose to present today an immediate practical plan of organization to attack the problem of price rigidity by freeing competitive forces. It is a program

[10] Thurman W. Arnold, Assistant Attorney General, Department of Justice, Washington, D.C. Testimony before the Temporary National Economic Committee, December 8, 1939. Hearings. 76th Cong. 2d session. Part 21. p. 11311-13.

which could be started in a week's time without further legislation, provided sufficient funds and personnel were available.

This plan of organization has four principal objectives:

1. To make the voice of consumers an effective force as a counter balance against pressure groups.

2. To prevent the unreasonable use by aggressive groups of the necessary privileges of collective action, granted by Congress or the common law to agriculture, labor, and business.

3. To attack unjustified price increases in one industry at a time in the light of the specific problems of each industry.

4. To provide access to the legislature for such special problems of business, labor or agriculture which demand special treatment or regulation in the light of their particular facts and which cannot be reached under existing laws.

The demand for such an organization has been intensified by the recent war. Dr. Lubin in his testimony at this hearing indicated that in the absence of any regulatory action price rises already begun will continue; that the cost of living will increase, bringing with it demands for increased wages; that the result will be the same severe economic repercussions that occurred 20 years ago—an economy with widely expanded industrial facilities and increased agricultural acreage resulting from price advances—an expansion financed at inflated values with the consequent burden of high fixed charges and mortgage indebtedness; that the burden of these fixed charges upon agriculture and industry imposed a long period of readjustment which was reflected in the depression of 1921, and constituted an important factor in the depression of the thirties.

Dr. Lubin's testimony also shows conclusively that the dislocation of prices does not occur by any general rise in all industries, but rather by the aggressive and inflationary action of groups of particular industries immediately stimulated by the war.

The conclusion is obvious. It is not general remedies we need but the application of a flexible instrument which is capable of taking up one industry at a time. Our proposed plan of organization is based on the premise that such a flexible instrument can be found in the Sherman Act if it is properly coordinated with other activities of government.

The Sherman Act does not attack unjustified profits of individuals. It concerns itself only with the activities of organized groups. It is effective because production and distribution in this country are operated by organizations and not by individuals. It is flexible because it judges the reasonableness of each organization by its performance.

The Sherman Act can become an effective instrument of price control if the following essential conditions are met:

1. A study of business, industry by industry, giving consideration to all pertinent facts relating to each industry.

2. Investigation of each industry in its entirety, rather than piecemeal.

3. Easy contact by consumers of regulatory representatives so that complaints of consumers may be made articulate and form the basis for proper investigation. Effective consumer representation must be created in determining price policies.

4. Creation of an agency or tribunal before which hearings may be conducted in situations wherein existing laws are inadequate, or in which conflicting decisions require immediate legislative clarification, or in which enforcement of the antitrust laws would result in destructive competition.

Such a tribunal should not be an agency with unexplored power and without experience in dealing with business problems. It can be set up within the present governmental framework by coordinating the activities of the existing governmental bodies which are especially devoting their attention to the freeing of competitive forces. These organizations are the Antitrust Division, the Federal Trade Commission, and the Temporary National Economic Committee itself. They must be geared to work not only with each other but also with consumers' organizations and trade associations in industry.

PROGRAM FOR THE WAR AND FOR THE YEARS TO FOLLOW [11]

If it is true that the primary consideration is greater production—armament first and civilian second—then a question arises as to whether our enthusiasm for price fixing does not need to be tempered considerably and its possible or probable consequences examined with greater care. If it can be demonstrated that price fixing impairs production where a rise in prices would expand it, then we are faced with the question of which is of greater importance—increased production or stable prices. In every case I should urge greater production as the primary consideration.

It is my impression that common and almost general praise of price fixing in this country today concerns itself chiefly with the extent to which prices have not risen, and that it practically never shows any concern or knowledge as to whether production has increased or decreased or is impaired or dislocated, or as to what other unfortunate consequences exist or are invited.

Unless we watch this matter of price fixing more carefully, and concern ourselves more with an increase in production and less with the stability of prices, I fear that this nation may learn once again, and with very serious consequences, an old lesson regarding the evils of government price fixing. We seem to have forgotten that the lessons of experience teach that price-fixing efforts of governments, except as a means of regulating monopolies, constitute one of the black chapters in human history—a chapter that is replete with instances of man's extreme inhumanity to man.

We seem to be paying insufficient attention to the fact that prices are fundamentally indicators recording the state of supply and demand, and that tampering with an indicator, while the

[11] By Walter E. Spahr, Professor of Economics, New York University. *Controller.* 10:214-23, 229. May, 1942.

forces of supply and demand are distorted, is equivalent to manipulating a thermometer or tying down a safety valve which is supposed to let off an excessive amount of steam and to act as a warning or guiding signal. Furthermore, price fixing of the type commonly proposed today tends to point toward a repression, not an expansion, of production. It invites a distortion of supply and demand, priorities, dislocations, bankruptcies, subterfuges, substitution of inferior qualities and materials, black markets, licensing, rationing, penalties, cheating, lying, crime, government buying and selling, a rampant bureaucracy, government inspection and supervision everywhere—the possibility of our nation being plunged into a state of moral, ethical, and economic degeneration and degradation.

How any one can demonstrate that the sad consequences, resulting from widespread price fixing by our government, will not exceed those experienced in a sharp rise of prices and a probable subsequent reaction is not clear, nor are serious attempts being made to demonstrate how these assumed greater gains are assured. We have apparently simply assumed that price fixing will bring more benefits than harm. Much, if not practically all, of the current agitation for price fixing appears to rest upon fears, hopes, guessing, and wishful thinking rather than upon the lessons of experience. What it is in human experience or the principles of economics that warrants the current insistence upon price fixing is not clear to me, and I do not think that the advocates of price fixing make this clear. The fact that other nations are now trying price fixing on a large scale does not, in my opinion, prove that it is a wise undertaking.

Increased production, in the heavy goods industries under pressure of the war demand for these goods, causes rising prices. These rising prices in many if not most of these instances induce greater production, direct goods and services into these channels in which demand is most intense, increase employment, and produce greater income and more taxes for the government. These are natural and proper sequences, and they should be interfered with only with the greatest care if we really wish to do first things first. In our attempts to block these natural sequences we may find to our dismay that we are meddling with economic principles which should have been capitalized as a means of strengthening ourselves in our efforts to win this war and to win it quickly.

When it can be demonstrated that sharply rising prices, because of absolute scarcities, cannot induce greater production, it might possibly be the case that the economy to the government, due to price fixing in these instances, will yield a greater social gain than loss. This probably is true in the case of some of our strategic and absolutely scarce war commodities. But even in these instances great care should be exercised lest serious mistakes will be made. A sharp rise in prices of every scarce or absolutely scarce goods might induce substitutes to appear which might not be foreseen. Furthermore, a sharp rise in prices tends quickly to force people to forego the purchase of these unusually scarce goods, and the higher prices should yield higher profits which should produce more revenue for the government. The common argument that unless we have price fixing and rationing the rich will grab these high-priced scarce goods is not weighty in the face of the more important considerations—namely, greater production and the winning of the war as quickly as possible, plus the evils and costs of price fixing and rationing.

Scarcity is merely a relative thing; so long as any goods commands a price it is scarce. Therefore the currently popular notion that prices should be fixed because certain goods are very scarce finds no good support in economics. And even in the case of absolutely scarce goods support for price fixing on these particular grounds is lacking. Such support must be found on other grounds, and they are of a highly questionable character.

Since we embarked upon our program of price fixing, how often have we read such statements as the following from *The*

New York Times (Dec. 13, 1941): "The figures for production of copper so far this year indicate that in that industry when prices are frozen, production also is frozen"? Or, as one observes the great supply of scrap iron and steel lying unused throughout this country, in the face of the government's constant stressing of the scarcity of iron and steel, how can one assume that if prices were sufficiently high this waste scrap would not be drawn into use?

It impresses me as a peculiar thing that so many people who have vigorously fought for preservation of economic and political democracy in this country have demanded, and are now demanding, with equal or greater vigor, widespread price fixing which would involve a bureaucracy and a plague of government agents, inspectors, and auditors that would exceed a Communist's wildest dreams. Furthermore, when government agents of the "economic-planning" type obtain power over goods and private enterprise, imaginary "scarcities" appear overnight. That has already revealed itself in this country, and should, I think, provide important lessons for those who are more concerned with increasing production than in giving some bureaucrat an opportunity to try to justify his position and salary and to revel in the "glories" of power over private enterprise. It also should be observed that apparently all Communists, Socialists, "planners," and radicals want price fixing. And why shouldn't they want it since it can provide them with a field day in which to bring private enterprise to its knees and to grind its nose into the ground at their feet? Let the ardent advocate of price fixing read, regarding Britain's sad experience with it, "The Moral Rot," in *The Statist* (August 30, 1941), which relates what is after all an old and universal story.

I am confident that we are not giving sufficient attention to this black side of price fixing; and I think we would do well to be far more careful and circumspect in our considerations of the use of this very dangerous device.

WARTIME PRICE CONTROL AND THE AMERICAS [12]

This war, in its economic phases, is a series of battles. Essential to military victory are the battles for production of arms, to move supplies to the fighting fronts, to mobilize the resources of the Americas behind the fighting men.

Now, too, another great economic battle is being fought. This is the fight to control prices, to keep living costs from rising sky high. It is an effort to prevent another war-born cycle of inflation and deflation. This battle against inflation is being waged in the interest of consumers throughout the Americas.

For price control is not the concern of the United States alone. The economies of the Americas have become more closely interrelated than ever. When prices rise in the United States, the influence upon price levels in our neighboring republics is widespread. That has been demonstrated amply since the war started in 1939.

The common interest of the Americas in wartime price control was recognized at the Rio de Janiero Conference of American Foreign Ministers last January. Representatives of other American republics at Rio remembered all too vividly the disastrous consequences of the violent cycle of rising prices and post-war collapse generated by the First World War. The Rio Conference, like wartime planning in the United States, was moved by an urge to profit from the lessons of the past.

Consequently, the United States has undertaken to extend the protection of its price controls to all the Americas. Sumner Welles, the Under Secretary of State, stated at the Rio Conference that this country would apply price control to exports destined for the other American republics.

[12] By Seymour E. Harris, Chief, Export Price Control, United States Office of Price Administration. *Foreign Commerce Weekly.* 8:12. July 11, 1942.

PERMANENT PRICE CONTROL POLICY 67

Late in April came comprehensive action covering export prices. All exports were brought under price control. Previously only selected items were subject to such regulation, in the same manner as the selected control exercised over domestic prices.

Here was another application of the basic United States policy of equality of treatment for the Americas. This equal-treatment policy is being followed in the sharing of strategic and critical materials, in rationing of manufactured goods, and in other wartime regulations.

In actual practice, what equality of price treatment means is this: Exporters within the jurisdiction of United States government controls may charge no more than the domestic price ceilings, plus legitimate expenses of doing export business on a reasonable profit margin.

The Maximum Export Price Regulation is an attempt to control export prices in the same manner as general price control within the United States. Internally, this effort at checking rising living costs has widened to cover virtually everything the consumer eats, wears, and uses.

In figuring prices, the exporter may add a premium to cover his overhead expenses and margin of profit. This premium is defined as the lower of the premiums earned in two periods: the second half of 1940 or from March 1 to April 15 of this year.

The reason for selecting these periods is that export prices on the whole were rather high in 1941. Therefore, it was necessary to go back to 1940. In some instances, however, 1940 prices were not available. So it was necessary to provide also the 1942 base. Included among expenses which may be added to export prices are such costs as war-risk insurance and extraordinary transportations charges.

The United States Office of Price Administration tries to give the exporter a fair deal. It wants to keep goods flowing to the other Americas, to facilitate inter-American trade.

Now that the other American republics are dependent largely upon the United States for many important materials and factory-made goods, it is doubly important to keep the machinery of trade going smoothly. It would be a mistake to reduce prices below the level necessary to move goods.

So where it can be shown that the Export Price Regulation fails to allow sufficient premium to keep goods moving, the Office of Price Administration is open to changes which will keep trade going. This does not mean, however, that the Office of Price Administration determines the volume of exports. But it does mean that it aims to prevent so far as possible excessive price-boosting on exports destined for our Good Neighbors. It is the Office of Price Administration's job, moreover, to regulate prices with the objective of getting free movement of the materials and manufactured goods considered essential to the economies of the other Americas by the War Production Board, the Board of Economic Warfare, Lease-Lend and other agencies. These agencies are studying requirements of the hemisphere markets in the light of over-all distribution of supplies for war industry, lend-lease, and essential civilian requirements in the United States.

Altogether the combined demand is tremendous. Even the huge industrial capacity of the United States is inadequate to fill all orders. Hence there is therefore need for government action to prevent speculators from running away with prices. Without government protection, users of many essential goods might find themselves at the mercy of wartime profiteers.

Price control in the United States will not automatically solve all trade problems of the other Americas. Nor will it assure stabilized living costs throughout the hemisphere. It is simply one approach.

Regulation of prices down to the ultimate consumer in the other Americas implies cooperation among the countries of this hemisphere. United States price controls cannot guarantee stable prices after scarce goods get out of the hands of dealers and merchants beyond the reach of the Office of Price Administration.

To get full benefit of Untied States controlled prices, the other American republics likewise must attempt to limit profiteering. There must, in other words, be coordination of price control between the United States and the other Americas— mechanisms of price control in our neighboring republics as well as in this country.

This need of cooperation in controlling prices and rising living costs is being recognized more widely. Many newspapers in South and Central America have become aware of it and have raised voices in behalf of price control in their own countries. This is encouraging.

What is at stake is well worth the cost of such cooperation. For rising living costs may rob the worker of the fruits of his labor, deprive the Americas of the benefits of higher money income, and set the stage for another post-war business collapse. The best indication that the Americas mean to prevent these evils is the tendency to cooperate in making price control work on a hemispheric scope.

ANTI-INFLATION PROGRAM [13]

Every American working for wages is personally and vitally concerned in the nation's effort to avert inflation. Every wage earner is equally concerned in the nation's wage policy and the effect of this policy on the workers' contribution to maximum war production.

Every American worker will do his very utmost to help his country win. But he will insist that our common sacrifice be equal, fair and just. To assure equality, fairness and justice to all in the war effort, the American Federation of Labor offers the following program of inflation control:

[13] *American Federation of Labor Weekly News Service.* 32:1. July 21, 1942.

1. Wage adjustment through the process of collective bargaining between labor and management.

All disputed wage issues, except those covered by wage stabilization agreements, shall be settled by (a) direct negotiation, (b) conciliation and arbitration, and (c) submission to the National War Labor Board for final decision.

2. Voluntary wage stabilization agreements.

Voluntary wage stabilization agreements are now in effective operation in the shipbuilding and construction industries, covering more than 2,500,000 workers. Voluntary wage stabilization agreements shall be negotiated and executed in other key industries and occupations with wage stabilization boards established in each, similar to the boards now in operation.

3. Wage Policy Commission.

A Wage Policy Commission shall be established consisting of an equal number of representatives of labor, management and the government, to coordinate and unify wage policies and to prescribe such agreed policies to all government agencies whose activities are related to wage adjustment directly or indirectly.

4. Payment of wage increases in war bonds, cashable after the war.

Future wage increases for the same work shall be paid in whole or in part in a special series of war bonds not convertible into cash until after the war, except in distress situations. The use of such bonds will prevent dislocation of our wage structure and will enable workers to build up a reserve of buying power to be released after the war to sustain our economy and prevent unemployment when the armed forces and war industries are demobilized.

5. Immediate application of effective control of excessive corporate profits through taxation and through integrated cost control on all government purchasing.

6. A program of progressive income taxation designed to prevent personal profiteering in wartime, and increase contribu-

tions for an extended social security program with wider coverage which would give the mass of our wage earners a measure of economic security when war employment ends.

7. Voluntary contribution by all citizens to the cost of winning the war by largest possible investment of their earnings in war bonds.

8. Effective control of prices on consumer goods at the retail, wholesale, and manufacturing levels, and control of rents.

9. Rationing of all scarce commodities to distribute them fairly among all and to prevent profiteering and hoarding.

10. Price ceilings on materials and equipment produced on government account cannot and will not keep down the cost nor eliminate profiteering in war production. Price ceilings on war contracts tend to retard war output. They are inflexible, unrealistic, and cumbersome to administer. In expanded production unit costs are constantly reduced and military specifications are constantly changing. Maximum economy in government spending for war goods, combined with maximum output and maximum speed, can only be achieved through unified cost control. We recommend that the necessary technical service be established in the Executive Office of the President to direct and unify cost control in all procurement and war production agencies.

On April 27 the President of the United States laid down a seven-point program to control the cost of living. The program called for stabilization of profits; stabilization of wages; and stabilization of farm prices. It also provided for ceilings on prices of consumer goods and rents; purchase of war bonds; rationing; and credit curtailment. The President told the nation that the cost of living can be stabilized only if profits, wages and farm prices are stabilized at the same time. He said "The important thing to remember is that each one of these points is dependent on the others if the whole program is to work." This he laid down as the essential principle of equality of sacrifice, of equality of privilege for all to work for victory of democracy by democratic means.

To date this principle has been disregarded. Only wages are being submitted to control. Exorbitant personal and corporate profits from war production are daily reported in the press. Even greater profits are concealed by clever accounting devices. Food prices continue to rise. There are no price ceilings on some 25 farm commodities.

Labor must not be made the scapegoat for the administrative deficiency in inflation control to date. There must be one unified policy of inflation control equally applied to all groups and enforced by active and free participation, willing and understanding, on the part of the people themselves.

Labor will accept wage stabilization which is accompanied by stabilization of profits and other income payments. Labor insists that wage stabilization be achieved not by arbitrary decree but by agreement. Wage stabilization must not preclude correction of substandard rates, elimination of inequalities, nor adjustment of rates to compensate for increased skill and output.

The American Federation of Labor proposes the above program as a constructive and workable plan of inflation control under which democratic procedures will be safeguarded, collective bargaining will continue to be the major instrumentality of wage stabilization and cost of living will become firmly anchored.

Labor can and should be a responsible partner in winning the war. The adoption of our plan will enable American workers to increase speed and productivity of war industry as free and willing citizens striving mightily for victory of democracy over dictatorship and enslavement.

EMERGENCY PRICE-CONTROL ACT [14]

Summary

After several months of discussion, the Emergency Price-Control Act of 1942 (Public, No. 421) was passed by Congress

[14] *Monthly Labor Review.* 54:794-9. March, 1942.

PERMANENT PRICE CONTROL POLICY

and approved by the President on January 30, 1942. It became effective immediately, and will remain in effect until June 30, 1943, unless sooner terminated by executive proclamation or by concurrent resolution of Congress. The purpose of the act is to check speculative and excessive price rises, price dislocations, and inflationary tendencies.

The Price-Control Act vests in a single administrator the power to establish maximum prices for all commodities except farm products and to control rents in defense areas. In the case of farm products, maximum prices may not be established until prices for agricultural products have reached the highest of four levels, the most important of which is 110 per cent of the parity prices established by the Secretary of Agriculture. After this level is attained, the Administrator may fix the prices of farm products, subject, however, to the approval of the Secretary of Agriculture.

In addition to his price-fixing powers, the Administrator is authorized to regulate or prohibit hoarding and speculative or manipulative practices likely to result in price or rent increases. He is also authorized to enter into voluntary agreements with producers, processors, manufacturers, retailers, wholesalers, and other affected groups for the purpose of fixing maximum prices. When maximum production of a commodity is not being obtained, the Administrator may buy and sell commodities and subsidize domestic producers.

As an aid in the enforcement of the law, the Administrator is authorized to license wholesale and retail dealers in any commodity, and, through court action, to revoke licenses for violation of the act. The Administrator may also enjoin the violation of the act in an appropriate court and, in addition, noncommercial buyers are authorized to bring an action against a seller for triple damages, or $50, whichever is greater. Willful violations are punishable by fine and imprisonment.

Administration of Act

The act establishes the Office of Price Administration, under the direction of a Price Administrator who is appointed by the President with the advice and consent of the Senate. The Administrator is empowered to issue subpoenas and to require dealers in commodities and owners of rental property to make reports and furnish information under oath. Information which the Administrator deems to be confidential or which is requested to be treated as confidential may not be disclosed, unless he determines that witholding it is contrary to the interests of national defense.

Control of Commodity Prices

Whenever the Administrator finds that the prices of commodities have risen or threaten to rise, he may establish such maximum prices as in his judgment will be generally fair and equitable. As far as practicable, in establishing any maximum price, the Administrator is to ascertain and give due consideration to the prices prevailing between October 1 and October 15, 1941, and make adjustments for speculative fluctuations, general increases or decreases in cost of production, distribution, and transportation, and in the profits of sellers of the commodities involved. If there were no prevailing prices between these dates, or the prevailing prices are not generally representative, then the prevailing prices during the nearest 2-week period which are generally representative are to be used.

The Administrator is also empowered to issue temporary orders or regulations (effective for not more than 60 days) establishing as maximum prices the prices prevailing within 5 days prior to the date of the order. Before issuing an order or regulation, if practicable the Administrator is required to consult with representative members of the industry which will be affected by the order. In the case of any commodity for which a maximum price has been established, the Administrator shall, at the request of any substantial portion of the industry concerned, appoint an industry advisory committee or committees, either national or regional or both. At the request of the committee, the Administrator shall from time to time advise and consult with the committee with respect to adjustments of the established maximum prices.

Price schedules.—Any price schedule establishing maximum prices issued prior to the date upon which the Administrator takes office shall, from that date, have the same effect as if issued under this act until such price schedule is superseded by the issuance of a regulation or order. Such price schedules must be consistent with the standards and limitations contained in the act.

Rent control.—The Administrator is authorized to recommend the stabilization or reduction of rents for any defense-area housing accommodations within a particular defense-rental area. If within 60 days after the issuance of any recommendation the rents have not been stabilized or reduced, the Administrator may establish such maximum rents as in his judgment will be generally fair and equitable. In establishing any maximum rent the Administrator may ascertain and give consideration to the rents prevailing for the accommodations on or about April 1, 1941, and make adjustments for such factors as increases or decreases in property taxes and other costs. In special cases, he may consider the prevailing rents on earlier dates, but not earlier than April 1, 1940. In designating defense-rental areas and in establishing maximum rents, the Administrator may consider recommendations of state and local officials concerned with housing or rental conditions in any defense-rental area.

Maximum prices and rents.—Although generally the maximum prices and rents established by the Administrator are to be based on the rate prevailing at the time the order is issued, the Administrator is specifically authorized to establish a maximum price or maximum rent which is below the price or rent prevailing at the time the order was issued. The order may contain such classifications and differentiations and provide for such adjustments and reasonable exceptions as the Administrator finds necessary or proper.

Speculative practices and hoarding.—The Administrator is authorized, when he deems it necessary or proper, to regulate or prohibit speculative or manipulative practices or hoarding in connection with any commodity and speculative and manipulative practices or renting and leasing practices in connection with any defense-area housing accommodations, which in his judgment are equivalent to or are likely to result in price or rent increases.

Purchase and Sale of Commodities

Whenever the Administrator determines that the maximum necessary production of any commodity is not being obtained or may not be obtained during the ensuing year, he may, on behalf of the United States, without regard to the provisions of law requiring competitive bidding, buy or sell at public or private sale, or store or use, that commodity in such quantities and in such manner as he determines necessary to obtain the maximum necessary production. He is also authorized to make subsidy payments to domestic producers. However, in the case of a commodity which is defined as a strategic or critical material by the President, the determination is to be made by the Federal Loan Administrator, with the approval of the President, and in this case purchases, sales, and subsidy payments may be made only by certain corporations.

No sale or other disposition of any agricultural commodity may be made contrary to the Agricultural Adjustment Act of 1938. The law specifically provides that no maximum price shall be established for any fishery commodity below the average price of such commodity in 1941, and prohibits the regulation of wages in any occupation.

Agricultural Commodities

Special provisions are made in the act relating to maximum prices of agricultural commodities. No maximum price may be established or maintained below the highest of any of the following prices, as determined and published by the Secretary of Agriculture: (1) 110 per cent of the parity price for such commodity, adjusted by the Secretary of Agriculture for grade, location, and seasonal differentials, or, in case a comparable price has been determined for such commodity, 110 per cent of that price; (2) the market price prevailing for such commodity on October 1, 1941; (3) the market price prevailing for such commodity on December 15, 1941; or (4) the average price for such commodity during the period July 1, 1919, to June 30, 1929.

Parity prices are to be determined and published by the Secretary of Agriculture as authorized by law. In the case of any agricultural commodity other than the basic crops—corn, wheat, cotton, rice, tobacco, and peanuts—the Secretary is required to determine and publish a comparable price whenever he finds, after investigation and public hearing, that the production and consumption of such commodity has changed and has resulted in a price out of line with parity prices for basic commodities. In the case of commodities processed from agricultural products, it is provided that the maximum price for such commodities may not be below a price which will enable the producers to receive the established maximum price for their products.

No action may be taken under this act by the Administrator with respect to any agricultural commodity without the prior approval of the Secretary of Agriculture except in order to enforce compliance with any regulation, order, price schedule, or other requirements previously approved by the Secretary.

Prohibitions

The act makes it unlawful, regardless of any contract, agreement, lease, or other obligation, for any person to sell or deliver any commodity or to demand or receive any rent or to do any act in violation of any regulation or order made under the act. It is also unlawful for any person to remove a tenant from any defense-area housing accommodations or to refuse to renew a lease or agreement because the tenant is taking action authorized by the act. A person is defined as an individual, corporation, partnership, or other organized group of persons.

Enforcement of Act

Whenever in the judgment of the Administrator any person has engaged or is about to engage in an "unlawful act," he may obtain an injunction in the appropriate court. In addition, such person is subject to a fine of not more than $5,000 or to imprisonment for not more than 1 year, or both. A similar punishment is provided for a person who makes a false statement or entry in any document or report. In case of violation of a regulation, order, or price schedule, the person purchasing the commodity or renting the housing accommodations may bring an action either for $50 or triple the amount by which the consideration exceeded the applicable maximum price or rent, whichever is greater. If no person is entitled to bring such a suit, the Administrator may do so. This provision for triple damages will not take effect until 6 months after the effective date of the act. Furthermore, this provision does not apply in the case of a person who buys a commodity for use in the course of his trade or business.

The federal district courts have jurisdiction of criminal proceedings for violations of "unlawful acts," while both the federal and state courts have jurisdiction of all other proceedings which are not vested in the Emergency Court of Appeals.

Licenses.—In order to induce compliance with the law more effectively, the Administrator may require persons subject to any regulation, order, or price schedule to obtain a license as a condition of selling any commodity or commodities with respect to which such regulation, order, or price schedule is applicable. Licenses are not to be required for certain commodities, including newspapers, motion pictures, agricultural products, and fishery commodities. In case a person violates the provisions of the license or of the regulation, order, or price schedule after a warning is given of such violation by the Administrator, the license may be suspended by the appropriate court. The suspension may not be for a period of more than 12 months.

EXCERPTS

Can price enforcement, every bit as big as that of N.R.A. (different only in that this time the job will be to keep prices down instead of up), be any more successful than it was in 1935? (The problem will include policing the prices of 2,000,000 retail outlets, with fifty times as many customers, selling at least as many items for over $50,000,000,000, a year).—*Time. Ap.* 13, '42. *p.* 82.

The best-informed official view is that inflation will be controlled during the war, but that there is no assurance that it will be controlled when war ends. The reason is that, in war, government can do many things with or without specific Congress approval. In peace, the desire may be to get away from controls as soon as possible.—*United States News. Jl.* 31, '42. *p.* 17.

Labor does not want inflation; but it does want higher wages. Agriculture does not want inflation; but it does want "parity" prices. Business does not want inflation; but it does want higher income. Congress and the Administration do not want inflation; but, for political reasons, both hesitate to ask the country for the self-denial needed. All this suggests that, as a nation, we do not yet fully understand the problem, or are still unwilling to face the plain conclusions to which such an understanding leads.—*Editorial. New York Times. Jl. 26, '42. p. 6E.*

It is of the greatest importance to regulate the purchasing power of money and the debt-paying power of money from the standpoint of economic stability. There are many fixed prices in existence, such as railroad freight and passenger fares, such as express, such as charges for bus services, streetcars, postage, domestic services, vocational services, professional services, taxes, interest, debts, insurance policies, factory wages, telegraph and telephone, etc.

The creditor is entitled to receive the true value of what he loans, and the debtor should be required to pay not more than he borrowed in value.—*Robert L. Owen, former U.S. Senator. Congressional Record. Ja. 9, '42. p. A68.*

If we have inflation, the whole system of "social security" which we have been building up will become a mockery. At the inception of the social-security program certain malevolently inspired antagonists propagated the doctrine that the government's obligations would be directly repudiated when the time came to make heavy payments thereunder. This was an obvious canard. The government will without any doubt meet its obligations, in the accounting sense, but in the degree that inflation has occurred it will be repudiating them in fact. The people concerned will surely be more interested in the fact than in the form, and any such repudiation by subterfuge is, as the experience of Germany has shown, the open door to the most violent social disturbances.—*Frank D. Graham, Professor of Economics, Princeton University. Nation. Ja. 24, '42. p. 92-3.*

There is another reason for avoiding inflation, and it is a reason that may be more important than all the others because it involves the future peace of the entire world. After the war the United States will be forced to assume the leadership of the democracies in world affairs. That means that it must trade with the other democracies, and it will not be able to trade with them on an inflated price level. If American prices for industrial goods and other products are so high that other nations cannot buy them, then world reconstruction will be simply a beautiful dream that will not come true. There is more at stake here than most people realize, but Americans simply must understand these things if their country is to win the peace.—*Edward A. O'Neal, President, American Farm Bureau Federation. Rotarian. Ja. '42. p. 16-17.*

Consumers' cooperation is the permanent remedy for balancing price and income—for a nation as a whole and for each individual. Consumers' cooperation is the permanent remedy for inflation and deflation. We should turn to this permanent remedy and build cooperatives stronger and faster in America.

As Congressman Voorhis declared in a recent radio address:

The only reason we must use this remedy is because the people have not organized to protect themselves. If even 25 per cent of our American people were tonight organized into cooperatives, as more than a million of our families are now organized, we would not need government control of prices. Consumer cooperatives could do a better job of it as they have proven in other nations and in some cases in our own. And I pray God some day they will be strong enough to do this job without the necessity of governmental action.

—*E. R. Bowen, Editor, Consumers' Digest. Consumers' Digest. D. '41. p. 233.*

A second, and not less important, purpose of price control is to maintain some sort of economic parity among the various elements of the population. This problem is complicated by the fact that there never was any such equity. This gives every group that has powerful political influence a sense of justification for trying to better its relative position. But wartime is not the time to do it. The wisest word in the President's statement is this: "All bulwarks against inflation must fall unless all of us—the business man, the worker, the farmer, and the consumer—are determined to make those bulwarks hold fast." They will certainly fall if every group that can command a potent lobby is determined to improve its own position a little before permitting prices, wages and profits to be stabilized for the duration.—*Christian Century. F. 11, '42. p. 173.*

The fixing of the general level of prices merely fixes the purchasing power of the dollar. If we raise the general level of prices to that of 1926, it will mean that we have lowered the purchasing power of the dollar from its present expanded value to what it was in 1926. To fix the purchasing power of a dollar in this way is merely to fix the unit of measure for debts and for the business man's operations, exactly as we fix the yardstick, the pound, the kilowatt, or any other unit of measure. In other words, what the President is trying to do, after he has corrected the swollen dollar, is to make it thereafter a constant unit just as is the bushel basket or any other unit in commerce. . . .

It is claimed that stabilization of the price level is impossible by any means, monetary or otherwise. That has been not only disbelieved by monetary economists for years, but recently disproved by the experience of Sweden, which has maintained a stable price level for over one hundred weeks in succession, within .2 per cent at the maximum, and usually within 1 per cent. It is no accident that this has been done, and it demonstrates what we have always maintained, that it is possible to make the price level whatever we choose.—*Irving Fisher, Professor Emeritus of Economics, Yale University. Annals of the American Academy. Ja. '34. p. 130.*

A legislative compromise is reflected in Section 1(b) of the [Emergency Price Control] Act, which provides that the authority of the Act, and all regulations or orders issued thereunder, shall terminate on June 30, 1943, or upon an earlier date specified by Presidential proclamation or by concurrent resolution of the Congress. The provision for termination by concurrent resolution, although not without precedent in recent defense legislation, raises serious questions. If the issue be justifiable, a close question of constitutionality is presented. In any event, one may question the political wisdom of a device which, in substantial effect, deprives the President of his constitutional prerogative to exercise a veto power over legislation.

It is certainly to be expected that the authority of the Act will be continued beyond the specified termination date, June 30, 1942. Even if the war has been fought to a successful conclusion by the beginning of 1943, which now seems realistically improbable, the inflation which followed the First World War stands as an urgent warning that the brakes against inflation must not be taken off before a full return to a peacetime economy has been achieved. When the war is won, the tested tools of economic direction must then be turned to the winning of the peace.—*"Emergency Price Control Act." Law and Contemporary Problems (Duke University Law School). Winter, '42. p. 59.*

To place our emphasis on price-fixing, instead of on draining away excess purchasing power, is to ignore the basic cause of the disease and to try to cure only the symptoms. If excess purchasing power were removed, it would be necessary to fix price ceilings only on a few particularly scarce necessities, which would, of course, then be subject to rationing. In attempting to fix *general* price ceilings, while hardly touching excess purchasing power, the Administration has encouraged a quicker draining away of goods from merchants' shelves, and may soon find itself obliged to ration all sorts of goods that there ought to be no need for rationing.

The Administration and Congress must abandon the effort to apply different criteria to industrial prices and farm prices, and different principles of control to prices and wages. In his message of April 27 the President declared plainly that "we must *fix ceilings* on the prices which consumers, retailers, wholesalers and manufacturers pay for the things they buy." But he applied only the vaguer and ambiguous word "stabilize" to farm prices and to wages. This distinction cannot be made. Wages are the biggest single element in costs and prices. They must be treated alike or the system of control must break down. If wages are only to be "stabilized" then prices can only be "stabilized," but if prices are to be frozen then wages must be frozen.—*Editorial. New York Times. Jl.* 27, '42. *p.* 14.

It cannot be argued successfully that, since government subsidies are to be used to stabilize costs, at least prices will not have to rise. For cost is not the only factor that determines price. Supply and demand still count. If government is thus to augment the effective demand in the face of shrinking supplies the pressure to burst through price ceilings, legally or illegally, will be greatly intensified.

But there is still another fallacy involved, the cruelest fallacy of all. For government by subsidy to guarantee the farmer parity prices and the organized worker higher wages is a pretense of guaranteeing these two groups the maintenance or even the advancement of their living standards. But living standards are not determined by money. They are made up of the goods and services that money can buy. In the face of our shrinking supply of civilian goods it is inescapable, as the President himself has said, that as a nation our living standard must come down. Either the farmers and the workers are being offered a complete illusion or the rest of us are being sacrificed. These groups cannot maintain their living standards while the national living standards are being lowered, except at the cost of still further lowering the living standards of every one else.

The notion that government can evade its duty to come to grips with the problem of inflation by taking refuge in the familiar panacea of more government spending is dangerous in the extreme. If the Administration succumbs to this illusion it will lose the battle of inflation through sheer lack of courage to put up a fight. The fight against totalitarian aggression and the fight against inflation have this in common, they will never be won by appeasement. They will be won only by the utmost determination to work and sacrifice in a vital cause.—*Editorial. New York Times. Jl.* 15, '42. *p.* 18.

Ambitious organizers who are soliciting funds to fight rent control should not be permitted to repudiate the substantial progress that is being made to iron out inequities. These new overnight groups are attempting to use political coercion and threats. This is one form of protest which we will not countenance. We will not submit to the selfish aims of such groups. We will not submit to the weight of carefully promoted floods of telegrams. We will not submit to the synthetic pressure of staged mass meetings. . . .

We have tried to go first into those places where rent control was most needed, "into the key industrial centers where we are building ships and tanks and airplanes. We must have rent control in these areas because a stable labor supply is necessary to win the war. Workers cannot remain in places which do not offer them decent dwellings at fair rentals. . . .

In a few areas this movement assumes all the aspects of an old-time racket. Organizers are publishing notices in the press requesting landlords to contribute funds with which to fight rent control. In one city there are reports of the raising of a million dollar slush fund. And the promoters of this project threaten members of Congress with retaliation at the polls unless they use their influence to get rents raised in this key war production center. Obviously this effort at political intimidation will fail.

We have conducted careful investigations into the operation of rental housing in defense areas. And we find that, in general, owning real estate is at least as profitable now, even under rent control, as it was in the years before the expansion of the defense program.—*Leon Henderson, Federal Price Administrator, in radio address, July 16, 1942. New York Times. Jl. 17, '42. p. 6.*

Business men generally are eager to keep the price level as low as possible and to stabilize it to a point that is fair to the buying public. The purpose of the National Committee to Keep Prices Down is to solidify this general desire for reasonable prices so that the retail and wholesale outlets of all the nation's industries may join in a voluntary and patriotic effort to combat any trend toward higher prices.

The committee's program ties in with the public's antagonism toward unnecessarily high prices. The program also ties in with the views of those industrialists, financiers and economists who are opposed to a rising scale of prices and who are seeking a solution to the problem.

One of the aims of the committee is to cooperate with the government in its efforts to curb a rise in prices. It is the belief of the committee that every effort should be made by the public at large to supplement legislation to obtain the desired results.

The immediate plan of the committee is to enlist individuals and companies, representing all lines of business where goods are sold, each member striving to keep prices down in his own field of operation.

Nothing is more important to the nation's war program and to its determination to see that the Axis powers are defeated than that we should maintain a sound business structure. The movement to keep prices down, thereby creating a sound price structure, is fundamental to good business, not only now, but in the post-war period. Practically everybody is agreed as to the desirability of preventing a rise in prices, and all that is needed is unified action in order to put the idea into practice.—*Julian Goldman, President, Goldman Stores Corporation. New York. Women's Wear Daily. Ja. 16, '42.*

A series of far-reaching proposals to provide a sound foundation for post-war recovery and a new basis for world economy were made by Mr. L. St. Clare Grondona at a meeting organized by the Institute of Export, held at the Royal Empire Society, at which Sir P. Malcolm Stewart, Bart., occupied the chair. . . .

Mr. Grondona's plan is that the British government should establish a Price Stabilization Corporation to operate in relation to all the chief non-perishable products in the same manner as the Bank of England used to operate in relation to gold. A fair average price (to be known as the datum line) would be established for each product, and the corporation would buy at a price (say) 10 per cent below the datum and (thereafter) sell at 10 per cent above datum. . . .

Mr. Grondona . . . went on to show how his plan would apply with equal effect to many manufacturers of standard grade and constant utility, such as piece goods of many sorts and various types of iron, steel, and other metal goods, as well as to paints, chemicals, fertilizers, and many other commodities. He suggested that each should have its own datum line and that the corporation should be ready to buy at a price 10 per cent below this and to sell 10 per cent above it.

By such means, he contended, a wide range of secondary industries would be maintained constantly in full production of goods that were of real utility to this nation and to the world; and the purchasing power of all engaged in these industries would be kept at a uniform high level.

The speaker's final contention was that, just as all great nations in the past had adopted the gold standard in line with Great Britain, they would in due course all adopt the price stabilization plan which was wholly beneficial and not inimical to any legitimate interest, national or international.

This would mean that, ultimately, all currencies would be exchangeable for known quantities of standard utility products and, at that stage, there would be stability in foreign exchange to almost the same extent as when all great nations were on the gold standard.—*Great Britain and the East. Ap. 3, '41. p. 266.*

Some relief—primarily to producers—may be granted through payment of subsidies. The Office of Price Administration has had some experience with subsidies which encourage production without upsetting established ceiling prices. Last January, differential prices were established for lead, copper, and zinc. The Metals Reserve Company was directed to purchase all lead, copper, and zinc output beyond certain quotas at prices respectively 42, 41, and 33 per cent above their basic ceiling prices. Purchasers continue to buy at the ceiling price, the government paying the premium price as a subsidy to the producer. The merits of this type of subsidy are that the ceiling is not punctured, the bulk of the output is obtained at a price no higher than the ceiling price, and the supply subject to higher costs is encouraged.

In Canada, the Prices Board adopted subsidies for the maintenance of ceiling prices in the case of unabsorbable differences in the domestic price system, and also to compensate for differences between the home and foreign markets. The Commodity Prices Stabilization Corporation was created and provided with an advance of 10 million dollars from government funds. The cost of the subsidies amounted to more than 2 million dollars for the first 5 months. It is expected that payments will eventually exceed this rate, although the extension of control in the United States has made easier the Canadian efforts. Nearly one-half of the rise in the cost of imported leather is being met by a subsidy. Milk producers are receiving payments to encourage the output of dairy products. . . .

In Great Britain an elaborate subsidy system has been developed for keeping in check cost-of-living prices. The Ministry of Labour's cost-of-living index was less than 1 per cent higher in April 1942 than in April 1941. Large subsidies amounting to £125 million in 1941 were chiefly responsible for holding these prices down in the face of advancing wholesale prices.

Basic criteria will be needed to guide the granting of subsidies. In order to keep payments to a minimum, the administrator must first determine which commodities are essential and which may be foregone for the duration. Subsidies will be warranted only to maintain or increase the supply of essentials where production is being discouraged by the ceiling and in general they will be granted at the manufacturers' level.— *Charles A. R. Wardwell and Gerald J. Matchett. Survey of Current Business. Je.'42. p. 23.*

The President's seven points, and the extent to which they have been carried out, are as follows:

1. The government must tax heavily and, in that process, keep personal and corporate profits at a reasonable rate and low level. He wanted a $25,000 limitation on personal net income after taxes. The tax bill now before the House totals $6,144,-000,000, or $2,556,000,000 below the Administration goal. The $25,000 personal income limitation was rejected.

2. Over-all price and rent ceilings should be established. This has been done in general.

3. Wages should be stabilized. The efficacy of this portion of the program is debatable, but literal effect has not been given to the President's declaration to wage earners that "you will have to forego higher wages for your particular job for the duration of the war."

4. Farm prices must be stabilized at 100 per cent of parity, and restrictions on sale of government-held farm surpluses at market prices must be removed. Congress, led by the Farm Bloc, has refused to repeal the 110 per cent of parity provision in the Price Control Act.

5. Citizens should voluntarily put more billions into war bonds. A goal of $1,000,000,000 a month in war bonds was set up, beginning in July, and receipts in the first fifteen days were $436,000,000.

6. All essential commodities of which there is a scarcity should be rationed in order to insure fair distribution among consumers. Only gasoline and sugar have been rationed on a general basis thus far, and Mr. Henderson has declared that failure of Congress to vote sufficient funds for the O.P.A. would prevent planned rationing of other items.

7. Installment buying should be discouraged and payment of debts and mortgages should be encouraged. Federal Reserve Board regulations are carrying this point into effect.

At the O.P.A. there was no comment today on the steel wage increase, but officials said it was being studied with a view to determining what price ceilings might be punctured by general application of the N.W.L.B.'s formula and how much additional purchasing power would be added to the inflationary gap.—*New York Times. Jl.* 18, '42. *p.* 26.

One of the first factors which will condition the post-war adjustment will be the state of the price structure. It will be inflated, presumably until the end of the first short post-war boom; and no one can tell in advance how much. The sequel will take place under new conditions, including general acceptance of the idea of managed monetary systems, and a labor movement possessed of the greatest power it has ever had to resist the deflation of its part of the price structure. As a result, there is more than usual uncertainty whether inflation will be followed by a more or less corresponding deflation. Our price structure is likely to have to be more closely related to those of other countries than in the immediate past; but their price structures may do almost anything.

If our inflation is kept within very moderate limits, there may be a possibility that prices might be deflated while wages, in general, were not. Or a sticky wage structure might prevent full deflation of prices, and keep this country's price level out of line with those of other countries, to our disadvantage. This disadvantage might be neutralized by devaluation, unless the other countries followed suit or went us one better. If a large inflation is followed by a heavy deflation, the wage structure will have to give ground, though presumably to a less extent than prices. The disparity may naturally be expected to be greater than after the last war, on account of labor's greater strength, and therefore may have less favorable effects. The crucial question is whether this will increase real labor costs more than industry can successfully absorb and still maintain an adequate volume of employment. A final possibility is that governments faced by a crushing weight of debt will see to it that the burden is not increased by any post war deflation. This would, of course, mean partial confiscation of pensions and other fixed incomes. Past experience with the type of inflation that goes racing to infinity will probably preclude any deliberate resort to that method of escaping the burden of debt, though the temptation may be severe. All in all, there is a variety of possible outcomes, prominent among which are those involving an increase in real wage rates.

The avoidance of a reaction comparable to that of 1920-21 may depend on the extent to which the initial post-war boom impetus is controlled and spread out over a longer time. With luck and good management, it may pass without too much disturbance into the longer transition period, which may last in the neighborhood of a decade.—J. M. Clark, Columbia University. *American Economic Review. Supplement, Mr. '42. p. 6.*

Price-control legislation in the present emergency is clearly within the power to regulate the value of money, since it provides a means of stabilizing the general level of prices and of preventing inflation. The proposed legislation under consideration and the legislation which is required at the present time does not cover merely a particular commodity but embraces the entire price structure, in order to protect the general level of prices. A particular commodity is affected by the legislation only when its price is subjected to inflationary pressures which drive it above the general price level and thereby threaten the stability of the entire price structure. The value of the dollar is measured by its purchasing power in terms of the general level of prices. Thus this type of regulation is inseparable from the regulation of the value of money itself.

The comprehensive powers of the national government over revenue, finance, currency, and commerce are peculiarly appropriate to the protection of our entire economy from the dangers of inflation in the present emergency. A stable currency and the unquestioned credit of the United States are the foundation stones upon which a successful program of national defense must rest.

To the extent that the proposed legislation applies to goods in interstate commerce and to goods in related intrastate commerce, it can be upheld under the commerce power. Maximum price legislation designed to prevent inflation is patently an appropriate measure to foster and protect interstate commerce. Moreover, the commerce power may be relied on to support legislation which is also based upon the national-defense powers, see *Ashwander* v. *Tennessee Valley Authority* (297 U. S. 288), or upon the fiscal and currency powers, see *Norman* v. *Baltimore & Ohio R. R. Co.* (294 U. S. 240).

Recent decisions of the Supreme Court make it clear that even in normal times the commerce power will support the regulation of prices within the scope of the commerce power. This is established by *United States* v. *Rock Royal Cooperative Co.* (307 U. S. 533), upholding the validity of the Agricultural Adjustment Act of 1937 and the validity of the minimum prices fixed by the Secretary of Agriculture for sales by producers to handlers of milk moving, whether across state lines or wholly within the state, into New York. The Court held that price fixing was a type of regulation which was valid under the commerce clause, stating (p. 569-570):

> This power over commerce when it exists is complete and perfect. It has been exercised to fix a wage scale for a limited period, railroad tariffs and fees and charges for livestock exchanges.

—*David Ginsburg, General Counsel, Office of Price Administration, in brief submitted to Senate Committee on Banking and Currency, December 11, 1941. Hearings on H.R. 5990. p. 223-4.*

The third point, not generally considered in the discussion of price control, and of very great importance to us in the years to come, is that unless America has a low price structure when the war ends, we may win the war only to lose the peace.

When peace comes, as it eventually must, what will be our position at the peace table and in world trade? If ours is a high price structure, the lean and gaunt nations, which have learned to do without, even if defeated, will be able to undersell us in the markets of the world. The economic and social dislocations that would result in this country might destroy all of the freedoms for which we say we are fighting. With a low price structure, America can hold her own and demand as a price for economic collaboration just terms of peace.

If we have such a low price structure, we can insist upon living standards everywhere being raised so that our own shall not be destroyed, and we shall not be forced to undersell everybody. With higher living standards and wages, the purchasing power for fuller world trade will be provided. What greater preventive of war can you effect?

But with a high price structure we shall be powerless to write a peace treaty that will protect our own standards of living from attack by other nations. We will lose our foreign markets and to protect our homeworkers, will have to take refuge in artificially high trade barriers. The disparities between various segments of our economy, between farmers producing for export markets and industries producing for home markets, will be aggravated. We will be unable to provide full employment for all our workers. Such a situation created by our own lack of foresight and lack of planning might well wreck us.

If England falls and we be left to carry on against German domination, in the inescapable trade war that would follow, the higher our price structure, the weaker we would be. In economic war, a low price structure might very well be the deciding factor for victory.

So great are the stakes, there must be no compromise in drafting an effective program of price control. Since every price is a resultant of the combination of all other prices it is both unjust and impractical to regulate one segment of the industrial fabric while exempting or providing special concessions for other segments. . . .

Since the goal of price control is to maintain a stable, balanced relationship between all prices, why not keep that balanced stability when you have it? Why permit the "norm," when the law of supply and demand was working, to be disrupted and then scramble wildly to recapture piecemeal what we had in the first place? The question is, shall prices be determined by an administrator working under every conceivable pressure, or shall Congress, by placing a ceiling as of a given date, keep prices at a level earlier established by supply and demand?—*Bernard M. Baruch, Chairman of War Industries Board in World War I, in statement before House Committee on Banking and Currency, September 19, 1941. House Hearings on H.R. 5479. Pt. 2, p. 996-8.*

If we fail on this sector of the domestic front, whatever our success in the field, on the sea, or in the air, victory will be bitter. For of all the consequences of war, except human slaughter, inflation is the most destructive. This is true however we measure the effect of inflation, whether on national morale, war production, or dollar indebtedness.

Rising prices and increases in the cost of living bring misery to our people, cause industrial unrest, and undermine our unity. Since prices do not advance at the same rate for all commodities, and living costs tend to rise more quickly than wages, the burdens of war are haphazardly distributed, with the heaviest burden on the farmer, the salaried worker, the small investor, the pensioner, and the veteran, whose incomes cannot readily be expanded. Rising living costs mean labor disputes and spiraling wage demands. And the suspicion of profiteering causes discontent which hampers production as surely as the bombing of factories. Rising prices now foreshadow an inevitable and precipitate deflation later with attendant depression and suffering. Such prospects and fears are not matters of future concern only. They sap energy and morale now.

Rising prices limit production. For price uncertainties prevent future planning and long-term commitments which are an integral part of the industrial process. Moreover, the entire program of priorities and allocation of scarce materials is in large measure dependent upon price stability. The flow of goods through the priority system cannot be controlled if producers are subjected to the temptation of increased prices from other sources. Either the government and other vital consumers are forced to bid against nonessential users, or bootlegging flourishes in violation of priorities regulation. Anticipation of rising prices attracts speculators and induces hoarding. This not only causes prices to rise above the level justified by demand and supply conditions, but results in withholding of essential materials from war production.

Rising prices inevitably increase the cost of the defense program. It is estimated that out of a total expenditure of 31 billion dollars from 1915 to 1919, 13½ billion dollars is attributable to the World War inflation. Since the summer of 1940, price increases have already cost us about 2 billion dollars. With appropriations and expenditures swiftly increasing, the resultant cost of inflation and the ultimate burden of indebtedness may engulf us.

These prospects the committee cannot face with equanimity. We must make adequate provision to prevent their occurrence. Accordingly, in amending the House bill, the committee has sought to strengthen it. That bill, when we were not actually at war, might have sufficed. If the authority granted had proved inadequate, additional powers might have been sought and there might have been time to do so. But the swiftly moving pace of war, with evidences of inflation already apparent, leaves little time for the luxury of experiment. The need for price stability is urgent. The cost of living must be stabilized.—*"Emergency Price Control act of 1942." United States. Senate Report No. 931. 77the Cong. 2d session. p. 2-3.*

It is sincerely to be hoped that the decision will not be to establish all-over ceilings on retail prices. First, such an undertaking is, in our judgment, not necessary. Ever since the first outbreak of war in Europe, in September 1939, retailers have been conscious of the need of preventing anything like a runaway inflation of prices and there has been strong and effective organized cooperation to prevent such a thing and to keep prices down.

The success of this effort may be readily demonstrated by comparing retail price indices for the first two years of this war with the price indices of the first two years of the previous war. A comparison of retail price indices with wholesale price indices for the past two years also will demonstrate that something more than the ordinary lag between wholesale and retail prices is present. There is no way of accounting for this except that retailers have voluntarily averaged prices instead of directly and quickly following the market and have consciously dug in their heels and resisted price advances which have not seemed to them justifiable.

It also must be pointed out that the government census figures show there are 1,700,000 retailers in the United States. They do not all deal in the same merchandise but there is a great overlapping of items and merchandise lines as between different types of stores. The work of policing and enforcing any all-over price ceilings would be a task so tremendous that it would be foredoomed to failure. In all probability only those retail concerns which are large enough to be easy targets could be dealt with.

Although it may be natural at a time like this for governmental agencies to imitate regulations which have been established in other countries, it should be pointed out that there is danger in applying ready-made formulas from abroad in the attempt to meet the needs of the hour in the United States. In Canada, for example, all prices have been "frozen" but it should be remembered that the economy of the United States is vastly different and tremendously larger than the economy of Canada.

Also, all wages were "frozen" in Canada at the same time that prices were. There appears to be no intention to fix wages in the United States. With the exception of net profit, interest and royalties, practically all costs which make up the price structure are labor costs in one form or another. To "freeze" prices without at the same time freezing the elements which make up prices is impossible.

The bane of those countries in which strict regulation of goods and prices have been attempted has been the development of "black markets." The prohibition law is a typical example of what a "black market" can be. It means, of course, that the law-abiding, responsible business concerns will conform to requirements and that the racketeers will find rich new opportunities to profit at the expense of the consumer and legitimate business. After the experience with prohibition Washington should be particularly careful at this time not to create a new great crop of hijackers and bootleggers.

The National Retail Dry Goods Association, through its War Service Committee, gave a great deal of study to the matter of retail price control by O.P.A. and, with the backing of a number of other national retail associations, presented a simple and workable plan to the officials. This plan strongly advised against any attempt to fix over-all ceilings.

Instead, it recommended that any such price ceilings be on a selective basis and applied at the discretion of the administrator only where necessary. It was the conviction of the retailers that competition at the retail level and the cooperation of retailers in the purposes of the government would do more to keep prices at a proper level than any price control efforts by government.

It is worthy of note that when Leon Henderson appeared before Congress in connection with the Price Control Act he volunteered the statement that retailers by their voluntary efforts had "done a good job" in keeping prices down. The situation has not changed. They still are doing a good job and there appears to be no justification for such action as now is being discussed.—*Lew Hahn, General Manager, National Dry Goods Association. The Association. N.Y. Ap. 3, '42. mim. p. 1-3.*

BIBLIOGRAPHY

An asterisk (*) preceding a reference indicates that the article or a part of it has been reprinted in this book.

BIBLIOGRAPHIES

Johnsen, Julia E. Federal price control. p. 245-66. (Reference Shelf. Vol. 15, no. 4) H.W. Wilson Co. N.Y. Ja. '42.

Pamphleteer Monthly. 3:1-38. Je. '42. Postwar planning; a selected, annotated bibliography of free and inexpensive materials compiled from the regular listings in The Pamphleteer Monthly.

Summers, Robert E. Wages and prices. p. 207-19. (Reference Shelf. Vol. 15, no. 6). H.W. Wilson Co. N.Y. '42.

BOOKS, PAMPHLETS AND DOCUMENTS

Boston Conference on Distribution, 1941. 95p. Retail Trade Board, Boston Chamber of Commerce. Bost. '41.
Especially: Retailer and national defense. Fred Lazarus, Jr. p. 40-6; Bottlenecks of business. Thurman W. Arnold. p. 53-7; Price regulation and price fixing—European and American experience. Julius Hirsch. p. 61-4; War finance, taxation and prices. Melvin T. Copeland. p. 64-7.

Chamber of Commerce of the United States. Agricultural price control; an analysis of the Emergency price control act of 1942. 10p. The Chamber. Wash. D.C. Ja. 30, '42.

Consumers Union of United States. Inflation: what can we do about it? Need for effective price control. 16p. The Union. 17 Union Sq. W. N.Y. '42.

Dulles, John Foster. Peace without platitudes. 15p. National Peace Conference. 8 W. 40th St. N.Y. Ja. '42.
Reprinted from Fortune. 25:42-3+. Ja. '42.

Grether, Ewald T. Price control under fair trade legislation. 517p. Oxford Univ. Press. N.Y. '39.

Hahn, Lew. All-over price ceilings at retail level. 3p. mim. National Retail Dry Goods Association. 101 W. 31st St. N.Y. Ap. 3, '42.
Condensed. Commercial and Financial Chronicle. 155:1542. Ap. 16, '42. Retail price ceilings opposed by Ass'n.

Hansen, Alvin Harvey. Economic stabilization in an unbalanced world. 384p. Harcourt, Brace & Co. N.Y. '32.

Hansen, Alvin Harvey. Fiscal policy and business cycles. 462p. W. W. Norton & Co. N.Y. '41.

Harris, Seymour E. Economics of American defense. 350p. W. W. Norton & Co. N.Y. '41.

Harwood, E. C. Current economic delusions and their probable future effects. 112p. American Institute for Economic Research. 1200 Massachusetts Av. Cambridge, Mass. '38.

Henderson, Leon. Control of prices and inflation; address before National Farm Institute, February 21, 1942. 11p. The Author. Office of Price Administration. Wash. D.C. '42.

Hodgson, James Goodwin, comp. Stabilization of money. 238p. (Reference Shelf. Vol. 8, no. 7) H.W. Wilson Co. N.Y. '33.

Johnsen, Julia E. comp. Federal price control. 266p. (Reference Shelf. Vol. 15, no. 4) H.W. Wilson Co. N.Y. Ja. '42.

King, W. L. Mackenzie. Controlling the cost of living. 12p. Director of Public Information. Ottawa, Can. O. 18, '41.

Kingsley, J. Donald and Petegorsky, David W. Strategy for democracy. Section III, Campaigning for plenty. Longman's, Green & Co. N.Y. '42.

Knight, Bruce Winton. Economic principles in practice. 659p. rev. ed. Farrar & Rinehart. N.Y. '42.
Includes bibliographies.

Littell, John McGregor. Price control and inflation. 46p. mim. (Littell Digest no. 19) The Author. South Orange, N.J. '41.

Marget, Arthur W. Theory of prices; a re-examination of the central problems of monetary theory. Vol. 2. 802p. Prentice-Hall, Inc. N.Y. '42.

National Association of Manufacturers. Emergency price control act of 1942; analysis of the act and brief review of price schedules issued during past year. 23p. (Law Department Bulletin). The Association. 14 W. 49th St. N.Y. F. 5, '42.

Nourse, Edwin G. Between automatic and authoritarian price-making. 38p. (Pam. no. 31). Brookings Institution. Wash. D.C. '42.
Chapter 1 of forthcoming book Price making in a democracy.

Nourse, Edwin G. Free enterprise, price policy, and democracy. 34p. (Pam. no. 38). Brookings Institution. Wash. D.C. My. '42.
Chapter 5 of forthcoming book Price making in a democracy.

Pettengill, Robert B. Price theory; with an introductory supplement on production economics. 74p. University of Southern California. Los Angeles. N. '40.

Research Institute of America. Price control. 149p. (Analysis 21). The Institute. 292 Madison Av. N.Y. '42.

Shepherd, Geoffrey S. Agricultural price analysis. 402p. Iowa State College. Ames, Ia. '41.

Sorenson, Helen. Consumer movement; what it is and what it means. 245p. Harper & Bros. N.Y. '41.

Spahr, Walter E. Appraisal of the monetary policies of our federal government, 1933-1938. 72p. Economists' National Committee on Monetary Policy. 70 5th Av. N.Y. O. '38.

Steiner, William Howard and Shapiro, Eli. Money and banking. 790p. Henry Holt & Co. N.Y. '41.

Stepp, James M. Economics of price in the milk industry. 154p. (Report, Series B, no. 9). Bureau of Public Administration. Box 1667. University Station. Charlottesville, Va. '42.

Strover, Carl. Monetary progress, including complete mastery of business depressions, general unemployment and inflations. 319p. American Money League. Ashland Block. Chicago. '37.

Summers, Robert E., comp. Wages and prices. 219p. (Reference Shelf. Vol. 15, no. 6). H.W. Wilson Co. N.Y. Ap. '42.

United States. Senate. Committee on Banking and Currency. Emergency price control act; hearings on H.R. 5990, December 9-17, 1941. 560p. 77th Cong. 1st sess. Supt. of Docs. Wash. D.C. '41.

United States. Senate. Committee on Banking and Currency. Emergency price control act of 1942; report to accompany H.R. 5990. 28p. 77th Cong. 2d sess. Rept. no. 931. Ja. 2, '42.

*United States. Temporary National Economic Committee. Investigation of concentration of economic power; hearings May 10-12, 1939, pursuant to Public Resolution no. 113 (Seventy-fifth Congress). Pt. 8. p. 3283-3491. Problems of the consumer. 76th Cong. 1st sess. Supt. of Docs. Wash. D.C. '39.

Warren, George Frederick and Pearson, F. A. Prices. 386p. John Wiley & Sons. N.Y. '33.

Wolff, Reinhold P. Study of Miami grocery prices. 33p. (Bulletin of Business Administration). University of Miami. Coral Gables, Fla. '41.

Wright, David McCord. Creation of purchasing power; a study in the problem of economic stabilization. 251p. (Harvard Economic Series no. 72). Harvard University Press. Cambridge, Mass. '42.

PERIODICALS

Academy of Political Science. Proceedings. 19:423-30. Ja. '42. Wages and wage policy. Leo Wolman.

Academy of Political Science. Proceedings. 19:431-8. Ja. '42. Prices and the cost of living in two world wars. Frederick C. Mills.

Academy of Political Science. Proceedings. 20:11-22. My. '42. Problems of price control. J. E. Clark.

Academy of Political Science. Proceedings. 20:23-34. My. '42. Price and wage control in Canada. A. F. W. Plumptre.

American Business. 11:14-16. D. '41. What is going to happen to prices? Melchior Palyi.

American Economic Review. 25:471-86. S. '35. Just price in a functional economy. Bernard W. Dempsey.

American Economic Review. 26·Sup. 267-90. Mr. '36. Problem of prices and valuation in the Soviet system; with discussion. Alexander Gourvitch.

American Economic Review. 32:Sup. 1-12. Mr. '42. Economic adjustments after wars; theoretical issues. J. M. Clark.

American Economic Review. 32:Sup. 275-89. Mr. '42. Relations between wage rates, costs, and prices. Lloyd G. Reynolds.

*American Economic Review. 32:Sup. 404-15. Mr. '42. Effects of the war on price policies and price making. John D. Sumner.

American Economic Review. 32:Sup. 1-135. Je. '42. Papers relating to the Temporary National Economic Committee.

*American Federation of Labor Weekly News Service. 32:1. Jl. 21, '42. Anti-inflation program.

American Federationist. 49:18-19. Je. '42. Price control, rationing and organized labor. Leon Henderson.

American Journal of Sociology. 47:941-57. My. '42. Economic institutions; development during the 1930's. Gardiner C. Means.

American Mercury. 54:679-87. Je. '42. Thurman Arnold: prophet of prosperity. William Bradford Huie.

*American Statistical Association. Journal. 37:13-21. Mr. '42. Price fixing of agricultural products. Warren C. Waite.

Annals of the American Academy. 139:1-173. S. '28. Stabilization of commodity prices. Ed. by C. P. White.

Annals of the American Academy. 171:127-31. Ja. '34. Reflation and stabilization. Irving Fisher.

Annals of the American Academy. 221:9-16. My. '42. Extent of administrative regulation of economic affairs. Harold D. Koontz.

Antioch Review. 1:441-51. Winter, '41. How England controls inflation. Ernest Dale.

Barron's. 22:43-4. Ja. 12, '42. Canada pioneers in price control. Harry S. Moffatt.

Barron's. 22:6. F. 2, '42. Price controls and farm products.

Barron's. 22:3. Ap. 20, '42. Why of over-all price control. Christopher Vogel.

*Barron's. 22:3. My. 11, '42. Some effects of price control. Julius Hirsch.

Barron's. 22:13. Je. 15, '42. Holes in the price ceiling; how unseen prices are jacking up living costs in Canada. A. W. McKague.

Bread & Butter (Consumers Union of United States). 2, no. 18:1-2. My. 1, '42. Fight against inflation—government takes the offensive.

Bulletin of the Pan American Union. 76:89-90. F. '42. Some aspects of recent social legislation in Latin America.

Business Week. p. 52. My. 16, '36. Reckless interference; Patman-Robinson-Utterback-Borah-Van Nuys price-control legislation.

Business Week. p. 34+. Ja. 10, '42. Britain under price control.

Business Week. p. 68. Ja. 17, '42. Old parity policy.

Business Week. p. 17-19. F. 7, '42. Henderson wins; Wickard is playing ball.

Business Week. p. 31-2. F. 14, '42. Labeling required; O.P.A. sets top prices on sheets, etc.

Business Week. p. 15-17. Mr. 7, '42. O.P.A. moves into the stores; price-fixing and rationing at retail level taking form slowly.

Business Week. p. 36. Mr. 21, '42. Continental unity; Canada feels price-fixing job might be facilitated if U.S. would act simultaneously.

Business Week. p. 19-20+. Mr. 28, '42. OPA's police job.

Business Week. p. 47-8. Ap. 11, '42. Fair trade coup? Use of price maintenance setups by O.P.A. instead of base period.

Business Week. p. 88. Ap. 11, '42. What a freeze really means; general price, wage, and profit freeze, à la the Baruch plan.

Business Week. p. 46-8. Ap. 25, '42. Price pickle; Canadian business men hope relief will come when U.S. controls are set up.

Business Week. p. 14. My. 2, '42. Price freeze, what it is and how it works.

Business Week. p. 41+. My. 2, '42. Assist for Ottawa; price control program of U.S. expected to ease some of Canada's problems.

Business Week. p. 84. My. 2, '42. Putting the freeze in perspective.

Business Week. p. 27-30+. My. 9, '42. How the price freeze works; report to executives.

Business Week. p. 41-2+. My. 9, '42. How Canada did it; five months of control have shown what business faces here.

Business Week. p. 17-18. Je. 27, '42. Hidden inflation; long-margin lines or in lower quality.

Canadian Chartered Accountant. 39:385-96. D. '41. Price and wage ceilings—why? Background of Dominion government's policy of control of wages and prices.

Canadian Chartered Accountant. 40:83-91. F. 25, '42. Administration of price control. A. Maxwell Henderson.

Canadian Forum. 21:263-4. D. '41. Holes in the ceiling.

Canadian Journal of Economics and Political Science. 8:186-96. My. '42. Price ceilings and international trade theory. G. A. Elliott.

Christian Century. 50:1260-1. O. 11, '33. Price-control is a radical measure.

Christian Century. 59:172-3. F. 11, '42. Price control arouses hopes and fears.

*Christian Century. 59:623-5. My. 13, '42. America in revolution.

Christian Science Monitor Weekly Magazine Section. p. 4+. Je. 20, '42. Shop talk from the farm. Nelson Antrim Crawford.

Clearing House. 16:262-4. Ja. '42. One million votes for price control. Harry A. Becker.

Collier's. 109:40-3. Je. 13, '42. Why we won't have inflation. Julius Hirsch.

Commerce. 39:15-17+. Mr. '42. How to live under price controls. Urban A. Lavery.

Commerce. 39:16-18+. My. '42. Our controls over inflation. John C. Weigel.

Commercial and Financial Chronicle. 154:1346. D. 4, '41. Price fixing totalitarian. Robert M. Harriss.

Commercial and Financial Chronicle. 155:119. Ja. 8, '42. Campaign is launched to prevent rising prices; National Committee to Keep Prices Down.

Commercial and Financial Chronicle. 155:566. F. 5, '42. President criticizes farm price sections of price control act; doubts adequacy.

Commercial and Financial Chronicle. 155:584. F. 5, '42. Roosevelt signs emergency price control act; commodity ceilings planned to check inflation.

Commercial and Financial Chronicle. 155:673-5. F. 12, '42. Text of Emergency price control act of 1942.

Commercial and Financial Chronicle. 155:1149. Mr. 19, '42. Inflation and price control discussed by N.Y. Federal Reserve bank in annual report.

Commercial and Financial Chronicle. 155:1155. Mr. 19, '42. FDR warns inflation in advancing prices; text of address on anniversary of the administration's farm program.

Commercial and Financial Chronicle. 155:1449. Ap. 9, '42. OPA and BEW outline export price policy.

Commercial and Financial Chronicle. 155:1708-9. Ap. 30, '42. President outlines anti-inflation program; heavier taxation, price, wage ceilings; text of message to Congress April 27.

Commercial and Financial Chronicle. 155:1778. My. 7, '42. Calls sweeping price regulations of OPA on consumer goods too stringent, unenforceable. Carlton A. Shively.

Commercial and Financial Chronicle. 155:1785. My. 7, '42. OPA price order on commodities, services.

Commonweal. 35:333. Ja. 23, '42. Price floor and ceilings.

Commonweal. 35:404. F. 13, '42. Inflation and price control.

Commonwealth Club of California. Transactions. 34:190-231. Mr. 12, '40. Price fixing—pro and con.

Conference Board Economic Record. 3:564-8. D. 24, '41. Control of prices and wages—a Canadian experiment. F. Cyril James.

Congressional Digest. 13:1-32. Ja. '34. Will the Roosevelt gold policy raise the price of American products? With pro and con discussion.

Congressional Record. 86:(current) 2672-4. F. 20, '40. Price fixing in our American economy. Louis B. Ward.

Congressional Record. 88:8-9. Ja. 5, '42. Factual index to hearings before the Senate Committee on Banking and Currency on the Emergency Price Control Act (H.R. 5990), December 9-17, 1941.

Congressional Record. 88:68-90. Ja. 7; 99-136. Ja. 8; 165-94. Ja. 9; 217-52. Ja. 10, '42. Price control; debate in Senate on H.R. 5990.

Congressional Record. 88:A67-8. Ja. 9, '42. Dangers of inflation. Robert L. Owen.

Congressional Record. 88:A119-21. Ja. 13, '42. So, this is inflation. Raymond Nunnery.

Congressional Record. 88:A141-2. Ja. 15, '42. Changes in the purchasing power of the dollar always bring economic distress. Jerry Voorhis.

Congressional Record. 88:452-4. Ja. 19, '42. Legislative program of American Farm Bureau Federation.

Congressional Record. 88:A192-4. Ja. 20, '42. America at war; address before Economists' National Committee on Monetary Policy, January 15, 1942. Robert A. Taft.

Congressional Record. 88:A322-7. Ja. 28, '42. Price control; brief. David Ginsberg.

Congressional Record. 88:A1766-7. My. 4, '42. Wages, prices, and profits. Robert A. Taft.

Congressional Record. 88:A1909-10. My. 13, '42. Commodity prices. Harold A. Packard.

Congressional Record. 88:A2930-1. Jl. 14, '42. Price control. Walter M. Pierce.

Congressional Record. 88:A2932-3. Jl. 14, '42. Dangers of inflation. Jesse H. Jones.

Consumers' Cooperation. 27:230-4. D. '41. How to balance prices and income to prevent inflation and deflation. E. R. Bowen.

Controller. 10:148-51. Ap. '42. War finance and price control. Herbert F. Fraser.

*Controller. 10:213-23+. My. '42. Program for the war and for the years to follow. Walter E. Spahr.
  Same condensed. Commercial and Financial Chronicle. 155:1538-9. Ap. 16, '42. Price fixing flayed as one of black chapters in human history.

Controller. 10:224-9. My. '42. Standards for control of prices under price control act. David Ginsberg.

Dun's Review. 49:11-19+. D. '41. Canadian wartime price control. Jules Backman.

*Economic Bulletin. 3:1-32. D. 16, '41. Price-fixing and commodity control; testimony before the Senate Committee on Banking and Currency on the price-control bill. Benjamin M. Anderson.

Economic Journal (London). 51:507-12. D. '41. Merits and demerits of German price-control during the last war. Leon Zeitlin.

Economist (London). 142:148. Ja. 31, '42. Price stop policy in Europe.

Economist (London). 142:405. Mr. 21, '42. Control of prices.

Factory Management and Maintenance. 100:58-63. Ja. '42. Our fight against high prices. Leon Henderson.
  Also separate. Office of Price Administration. Washington, D.C.

Federal Reserve Bulletin. 28:200-1. Mr. '42. Price legislation; Emergency price control act of 1942.

*Federal Reserve Bulletin. 28:441-9. My. '42. Statement of considerations involved in the issuance of the general maximum price regulation.

Financial and Investment Review. 10:1-4. Mr. '42. Farmer and inflation. O. B. Jesness.

Forbes. 48:10-11+. D. 15, '41. Bernard Baruch on inflation. Homer H. Shannon.

Foreign Commerce Weekly. 5:8-94. D. 13, '41. Some details of Canadian price control policy, with special reference to imports.

Foreign Commerce Weekly. 6:4-5+. Mr. 7, '42. Machinery of Canadian price control. Avery F. Peterson.

Foreign Commerce Weekly. 7:32-3. My. 9, '42. New export price control.

Foreign Commerce Weekly. 7:12-14+. My. 23, '42. Subsidies in the Canadian price control.

*Foreign Commerce Weekly. 8:12. Jl. 11, '42. Wartime price control and the Americas. Seymour E. Harris.

Fortune. 15:111-13+. Je. '37. Prices: fixed or free? Hugh S. Johnson; Paul Hollister.

Fortune. 24:94-5+. O. '41. Where do we go from here? Economic democracy fails where political democracy succeeds; might redistribute government and business, with more power to both. Geoffrey Crowther.

Fortune. 26:60-3+. Jl. '42. General Max over the U.S.; price ceilings clamp down on some dynamite. John Davenport.

Fortune. 26:62-3+. Jl. '42. Canada under the lid; report on price ceilings. Bruce Hutchison.

Great Britain and the East. 56:266. Ap. 3, '41. Post-war economic reconstruction: proposals based on price stabilization; summary.

Harvard Business Review. 20 no. 2:184-98. [Ja.] '42. Retail price control. Victor Abramson and Charles W. Phillips.

Harvard Business Review. 20, no. 3:277-89. [Ap.] '42. Direct control of machinery prices. Joel Dean.

Independent Woman. 18:389+. D. '39. There ought to be a law; just how much government regulation and planning will make for widespread better living? Dorothy D. Cook.

Independent Woman. 21:135-6+. My. '42. X marks the morrow; interview with Stuart Chase. Josephine Nelson.

Industrial Standardization and Commercial Standards Monthly. 13:146-8. Je. '42. Price control requires standards. Leon Henderson.

Journal of Accountancy. 73:103-12. F. '42. Price control. Victor H. Stempf.

Journal of Accountancy. 74:11-17. Jl. '42. Accounting aspects of price administration. Herbert F. Taggart.

Journal of Business of the University of Chicago. 15, pt. 1:95-130. Ap. '42. War expansion and price inflation. S. H. Nerlove.

Journal of Home Economics. 33:699-702. D. '41. Inflation strikes home. Harriet Elliott.

Journal of Home Economics. 34:6-9. Ja. '42. Control of rent. Karl Borders.

Journal of Home Economics. 34:231-3. Ap. '42. Price of what? importance of standards in war economy. Carol Willis Moffett.

Labour Gazette (Canada). 42:571-3. My. '42. Comparison of price control in Canada and the United States.

Law and Contemporary Problems. 2:1-177. [Ja.] '42. Emergency price control act; symposium.

Magazine of Wall Street. 70:60-2+. My. 2, '42. 1942 earnings and dividend prospects in the face of freezing of profits, wages and prices. Ward Gates.

Michigan Law Review. 40:937-68. My. '42. Procedure in emergency price fixing. Paul B. Rava.

Mining Congress Journal. 27:44-5. O. '41. Governmental price policies. John E. Hamm.

Monthly Labor Review. 53:1392-6. D. '41. Control of wages and prices in Canada.

Monthly Labor Review. 54:54-5. Ja. '42. Price regulations in Canada.

*Monthly Labor Review. 54:794-9. Mr. '42. Emergency price-control act; summary.

Mountain States Banker. 37:9+. My. '42. Taking the mystery from inflation. John S. Sly; Harley F. Lutz; William S. Carpenter.

Nation. 158:557-8. D. 6, '41. Inflation wins; House's action in emasculating the price control bill.

Nation. 154:91. Ja. 24, '42. Inflationary spiral. Keith Hutchison.

Nation. 154:92-3. Ja. 24, '42. Congress can stop inflation. Frank D. Graham.

Nation. 154:152-3. F. 7, '42. Price-bill fiasco.

Nation. 154:629-30. My. 30, '42. Inflation under price control. Harold Mager.

Nation. 154:710-12. Je. 20, '42. Price ceilings, quality cellars. Ruth Brindze.

National Municipal Review. 31:249-53. My. '42. Canada regulates wages, prices.

Nation's Agriculture. 16:3-4+. N. '41. Farmer looks at price control. Edward A. O'Neal.

Nation's Business. 30:62+. Mr. '42. Price control on Main Street; how it will affect you.

Nation's Business. 30:25-6+. My. '42. Plans may deny us food. Lawrence Sullivan.

Nation's Business. 30:23-5+. Je. '42. O.P.A. calls the signals. R. L. Van Boskirk.

Nation's Business. 30:27-9+. Je. '42. Rations: war need or reform? Lawrence Sullivan.

Nation's Business. 30:15-17+. Jl. '42. Ceiling plaster is full of rocks. R. L. Van Boskirk.

Nation's Business. 30:33-4+. Ag. '42. Plainly visible to the shopper. Ellen Newman.

New Republic. 105:608. N. 10, '41. Will the farmers remember?

New Republic. 105:641-2. N. 17, '41. Republicans betray defense; block every attempt to obtain price control. Michael Straight.

New Republic. 106:100-2. Ja. 26, '42. Congress bungles price control.

New Republic. 106:357-8. Mr. 16, '42. England closes the gap; against inflation.

New Republic. 106:534-6. Ap. 20, '42. How to control prices. Charles R. Whittlesey.

*New Republic. 106:856-8. Je. 22, '42. Economic strategy in a democracy. Max Lerner.

New Republic. 107:7-9, 18-19. Jl. 6, '42. Wages and arguments; with editorial comment. Harold J. Ruttenberg.

New York Times. p. 15. Ap. 29, '42. Text of general maximum price regulation decreed by O.P.A. to control inflation; Henderson states reasons for price action.

New York Times. p. 18. Jl. 15, '42. Yielding to inflation; editorial.

New York Times. p. 18. Jl. 23, '42. What makes inflation; editorial.

New York Times. p. 6E. Jl. 26, '42. Nature of inflation; editorial.

New York Times. p. 14. Jl. 27, '42. Anti-inflation program; editorial.

New York Times Magazine. p. 5+. N. 23, '41. Planned economy, and/or democracy. Elliott V. Bell.

Newsweek. 19:42+. My. 4, '42. Economic clamps are drastic but not an inflation cure-all.

Newsweek. 19:48+. My. 11, '42. Patches in his price ceilings next on agenda for Henderson.

Printers' Ink. 198:15-16+. F. 6, '42. How federal price control will rule U.S. business. Arthur C. Fatt.

Printers' Ink. 198:30+. F. 13, '42. Price control difficulties bound to arise. Arthur C. Fatt.

Printers' Ink. 198:26+. F. 20, '42. Price control in Canada and what it may be here. Arthur C. Fatt.

Public Affairs: a Maritime Quarterly for Discussion of Public Affairs. 5:57-61. Winter '41. Canada erects a price ceiling. Stewart Bates.

Public Affairs: a Maritime Quarterly for Discussion of Public Affairs. 5:134-8. Spring '42. Wartime price control in the United States, 1940-1942. Jules Backman.

Public Utilities Fortnightly. 29:79-84. Ja. 15, '42. Menace of inflation: stake of the utilities in price control and other methods of preventing runaway costs. Ernest R. Abrams.

Publishers' Weekly. 129:1857-9. My. 9, '36. Price legislation in the United States; a brief review of efforts toward price maintenance.

Publishers' Weekly. 130:2296-301. D. 12, '36. Supreme court decision upholding fair trade laws.

Review of Economic Statistics. 24:75-86. My. '42. War-time price control and price movements in an open economy: Australia, 1914-20 and 1939-40. E. Ronald Walker and R. J. Linford.

Rotarian. 49:12-15+. O. '36. Dividing the benefits of science; should this potential wealth be distributed through low prices to the consumer, or through high wages to labor? Harold G. Moulton; G. F. Warren.

Rotarian. 59:15-17+. D. '41. Two plans for U.S. price control. Leon Henderson; Bernard M. Baruch.

Rotarian. 60:16-17+. Ja. '42. Ceilings on wages? Yes! Edward A. O'Neal; No! William Green.

*Sales Management. 50:20-2. F. 15, '42. Six biggest snags in the path of price control. Walter Mitchell, Jr.

Saturday Evening Post. 196:32. Ap. 12, '24. Government price fixing again.

Saturday Evening Post. 214:18+. Je. 6, '41. Canada did it; price-control program. Albert Gore.

Scholastic. 40:9-10. F. 16, '42. Enemy at our doorstep.

Scientific Monthly. 16:623-37. Je. '23. Food control during forty-six centuries. Mary G. Lacy.

Southern Economic Journal. 8:218-37. O. '41. Government price fixing in Italy, 1922-1940. Roman F. Pitt.

State Government. 15:11+. Ja. '42. Problems of price and supply in wartime. Leon Henderson.

State Government. 15:137-8+. Jl. '42. Constructive emergency tax program; price control and rationing are natural allies in war against inflation. John K. Langum.

Survey Graphic. 31:19-23. Ja. '42. Wage policies and price trends. Isador Lubin.

Survey Graphic. 31:85-6. F. '42. Wages and prices in all-out war; reply to I. Lubin. John M. Clark.

Survey of Current Business. 22:12-18. Ja. '42. Direct price control in Great Britain. E. R. Hawkins.

*Survey of Current Business. 22:19-26. Je. '42. Price ceilings and wartime control over the American economy. Charles A. R. Wardwell and Gerald J. Matchett.

Time. 39:18. F. 2, '42. Price non-control.

Time. 39:65-6+. F. 9, '42. Tale of three countries.

Time. 39:68-9. Mr. 2, '42. Worst is yet to come.

Time. 39:82+. Ap. 13, '42. Catalogue of fears.

Time. 39:79-80+. My. 11, '42. OPA victim no. 1.

Time. 39:61-2+. Je. 29, '42. Subsidies or else; core of price control from now on lies in subsidies.

Trusts and Estates. 74:351-5. Ap. '42. Road to rationing; results of price and wage control as shown by French experience. Roger Picard.

Trusts and Estates. 74:364-5. Ap. '42. Control of prices and inflation. Leon Henderson.

Trusts and Estates. 74:455-61. My. '42. Inflation control and the general ceiling plan. Jules Backman.

United States News. 12:24. My. 15, '42. President's farm price plan; approval by majority of press.

United States News. 12:30. Je. 26, '42. Mr. Henderson's stand on wage increases: guidance by awards of the War Labor Board.

United States News. 13:20. Jl. 17, '42. Why Leon Henderson and Congress disagree.

United States News. 8:16-17. Jl. 31, '42. Inflation: the facts behind new warnings; effective controls probable during war, with real test coming later.

United States News. 8:26. Jl. 31, '42. Mr. Henderson vs. the unions; how price administrator's influence is felt in pay negotiations.

United States News. 8:28. Jl. 31, '42. Should Congress freeze wages and salaries as a means of stabilizing the cost of living?

University of Pennsylvania Law Review. 90:675-701. Ap. '42. Price control in war and emergency. Jules Abels.

Vital Speeches of the Day. 8:286-8. F. 15, '42. Price control bill and the farmer. Joseph C. O'Mahoney.

Vital Speeches of the Day. 8:342-7. Mr. 15, '42. To date, and tomorrow . Leon Henderson.

Women's Wear Daily. Ja. 16, '42. Movement to keep prices down is fundamental to good business. Julian Goldman.
Also separate. 1p. The Author. Goldman Stores Corp. 440 4th Av. N.Y.

Yale Law Journal. 51:819-47. Mr. '42. Legal and economic aspects of wartime price control.

Yale Review. n.s.14:274-92. Ja. '25. Prices and profiteers. William Trufant Foster and Waddill Catchings.

Yale Review. n.s.21:503-19. Mr. '32. Failure of farm board stabilization. Charles P. Howland.

Yale Review. n.s.23:448-65. Mr. '34. Reflections on the new dollar. Edgar S. Furniss.

Date Due

DEC 3 1948			
MAR 5 1949			

Library Bureau Cat. no. 1137

UNIVERSITY DEBATERS' ANNUALS

E. M. PHELPS, Ed. *Cloth. Price $2.25*

Series of yearbooks, each a collection of representative intercollegiate debates on important questions of the day. Constructive and rebuttal speeches for both sides. Each debate is accompanied by selected bibliography and briefs.

Vol. XXVIII. 1941-1942.
Federal Incorporation of Labor Unions; A League of Nations; Military Training; Failure of Colleges to Meet Student Needs; A Federation of Democracies Based on the Churchill-Roosevelt Principles; A Federal Sales Tax; Compulsory Saving; Post-War Reconstruction; Western Hemisphere Solidarity; Civil Liberties.

Vol. XXVII. 1940-1941.
Industry Can Solve the Employment Problem; Conscription of Capital for Defense; Preservation of Democracy Through Decreased Government Control; Interstate Trade Barriers; Japanese Aggression; Union of United States and British Commonwealth of Nations; Regulation of the American Press; Compulsory Military Training; Strikes in Defense Industries; Western Hemisphere Defense.

Vol. XXVI. 1939-1940.
The Basis of a Lasting Peace; Shall the United States Enter the War?; Government Ownership and Operation of Railroads; Neutrality of the United States; Extension of Reciprocal Trade Agreements; The Third Term for President; Should the Roosevelt Administration Be Approved?; The Dies Committee; Civil Liberties; Labor; Foreign Affairs; Government and Business.

Vol. XXV. 1938-1939.
The Increase in the National Debt; The Anglo-American Alliance; Government Ownership and Operation of the Railroads; Alliance of United States, France and Great Britain Against Fascism; Have the Achievements of Science Brought Progress?; American Solidarity; The Problem of Unemployment; The American Newspaper; "Pump-priming" Should Cease; Government and Health.

Vol. XXIV. 1937-1938.
Democracy and Economic Prosperity; American Isolation from European Affairs; Protection of United States Citizens on Foreign Soil; Academic Freedom; Grades and Final Tests Subversive of the Aims of Higher Education; American League of Nations; Anglo-American Mutual Assistance Pact; N.L.R.A. and Arbitration of Industrial Disputes; Unicameral Legislatures; Uniform Marriage Laws; Regulation of Advertising.

Vol. XXIII. 1936-1937.
The Constitution a Menace; Government Ownership of Electric Utilities; Subsidizing College Athletes; Teachers' Oaths; Unicameral Legislatures; Economic Internationalism; Minimum Wages and Maximum Hours (two debates); Consumers' Cooperatives; The Present-day Family as a Social Institution; The Sit-down Strike.

Vol. XXII. 1935-1936.
A Written Constitution a Hindrance to Social Progress; State Medicine; Compulsory Military Training; Legalization of Sweepstakes; Admission of Negroes to State Universities; The Neutrality Policy of the United States; The Parole System; Admission of Hawaii as a State; Limitation of the Power of the Supreme Court (two debates).

Vol. XXI. 1934-1935.
Equalizing Educational Opportunity; An Evaluation of the New Deal; Social Services and Unemployment Relief; International Traffic in Arms and Munitions; Democratic Collectivism; The Agricultural Adjustment Administration; Collective Bargaining; Government Ownership and Operation of Public Utilities; Pacifism the Highest Form of Patriotism; Japan and Naval Parity.

Vol. XX. 1933-1934.
British System of Radio Control and Operations; Armed Intervention; Japanese Policy in the Far East; A Department of the Consumer in the President's Cabinet; University of Chicago Plan of Education; Economic Reconstruction; Increasing the Powers of the President; Socialized Medicine; Freer Trade; Problem of State Liquor Control.

Vol. XIX. 1932-1933.
Limitation by Law of Gifts, Incomes and Inheritance; Property Taxation for State and Local Revenue; British System of Radio Control; Safety-Responsibility Plan of Automobile Insurance; Voluntary Domestic Allotment Plan; Federal Regulation of Electric Power Utilities; Dictatorship Versus Democracy; Capitalism Has Broken Down; Peace Is Impossible Under Capitalism; Stimson Doctrine of Non-recognition of Territory Acquired Through Violation of Treaties.

Vols. XII-XVIII. available. Contents furnished on request.